Praise for Michael Gibson and
REAL LIFE LOVE

"So honest, and incredibly practical. This book is perfect if you want to learn how to have relationships that count."

—Gary D. Chapman, PhD, bestselling author of
The 5 Love Languages

"The time to learn to love for real is now. This easy, practical, but powerful message from Michael Gibson will breathe life into all your relationships."

—Christine Caine, founder of A21 and Propel Women

"The world could use more love these days—or at least a better understanding of what loving others means. That's Michael Gibson's goal in *Real Life Love*. He's seen firsthand what happens when we love like God loves—and he's sharing those lessons with you."

—Dave Ramsey, bestselling author and nationally
syndicated radio show host

"If you really want to learn to win with people, you need to first learn to win in your relationships. *Real Life Love* takes readers into the details of how to do just that."

—John C. Maxwell, author, speaker and coach

"In *Real Life Love*, Michael Gibson provides a practical blueprint for developing truly authentic relationships."

—Michael Hyatt, *New York Times* bestselling author

"*Real Life Love*—who wouldn't want that? Michael Gibson has given an incredible answer for the relationship crisis facing his generation. Grasp what he is saying. Take his principles to heart. And you will have the key to create loving relationships that last."

—Bob Goff, bestselling author of *Love Does*
and *Everybody, Always*

"This book by Michael Gibson is for individuals who long to examine how they do relationships. The aim of this examination is to imitate the way Jesus loved and honored others. Is there any goal more worthy? Loving and respecting others not only energizes others, it enables one to influence others as Christ did. What a great call and high privilege."

—Emerson Eggerichs, PhD, president
and founder of Love and Respect Ministries

"One of the greatest decisions you can make is to live a life dedicated to building something that will stand as a testimony for the generations ahead. Without question, Gary Smalley's legacy continues in the lives of his family, friends, and all those his incredible ministry has impacted over the years. His grandson Michael Gibson is a carrier of this legacy—inspiring readers afresh to embrace relationships and love as God created and called us to."

—Brian Houston, global senior pastor
of Hillsong Church

"There's not much that our culture is more confused about these days than true love. With down-to-earth wisdom, relatable anecdotes, and a faithfulness to Scripture's teaching, Michael Gibson examines what it looks like to enjoy thriving, healthy relationships rooted in genuine, Christlike love."

—Jim Daly, president of Focus on the Family

"Books, if they do their job right, challenge us, and move us toward a brighter future. *Real Life Love* goes a step further. This impactful book challenges us to take a deeper look at our relationships. You will never be the same."

—Chris Hodges, senior pastor of Church of the Highlands and
author of *Fresh Air* and *The Daniel Dilemma*

"*Real Life Love* is full of timeless wisdom packaged and communicated in a timely way. It's a beautiful reminder that we are first called to love Christ, and that primary calling changes how we love our spouse in every significant way."

—Ryan & Selena Frederick, co-founders
of FierceMarriage.com

"We are all designed with a deep desire to be loved and to care for others. However, we often experience that when the first disagreement or loss happens, the sheen wears off and we don't have the skills to know how to regain the connection. Michael Gibson has thought through how this can work the right way, with sound principles and a fresh look at how relationships really work. Highly recommended!

—John Townsend, PhD, *New York Times*
bestselling author of *Boundaries*

"*Real Life Love* is guaranteed to have a positive effect on you and your primary relationships. Soak in Michael's wisdom and watch it serve as a tipping point for growth and meaning in your life and relationships."

—Doug Fields, bestselling author of *7 Ways to Be Her Hero*
and *Your First Few Years of Marriage*

"*Real Life Love* is a must-read for anyone who dreams of having vibrant relationships. Michael Gibson has done a wonderful job summarizing over fifty years of top-notch relationship wisdom into just seven simple principles. Dig in!"

—Jamie Ivey, author of *If You Only Knew* and
host of *The Happy Hour with Jamie Ivey* podcast

"We can't wait for our four young sons to be old enough to read this book! *Real Life Love* is masterfully written with humor, inspiration, powerful true stories, and timeless biblical wisdom. Its truths will help single people create a solid foundation for future relationships, and it will help those already in a dating or marriage relationship grow closer together. This is an excellent relationship resource, and we are already looking forward to reading Michael Gibson's next book!"

—Dave and Ashley Willis, bestselling authors and television hosts for MarriageToday

"If you're looking for a book that is both wise beyond its years and a fresh perspective on an age-old struggle—learning to love people well—then you've got to read *Real Life Love*. It's life-changing."

—Josh D. McDowell, author and speaker

"At the heart of every one of us there is a deep longing to love and be loved, but sometimes we get stuck. If you are frustrated with the relationships in your life, Michael offers a clear path to living differently, to *real life love*."

—Sheila Walsh, author of *It's Okay Not to Be Okay*

"*Real Life Love* is a gold mine of practical, time-tested relational nuggets that are immediately applicable. It's a thoroughly enjoyable read, and the generational wisdom here will enhance any relationship. If you don't want to settle for 'fairytale' or 'fools gold' relationships and want to enjoy the real deal, then read this book. Save yourself unnecessary headaches and heartaches. Read this book. You'll be glad you did."

—Gary J. Oliver, ThM, PhD, executive director of The Center for Healthy Relationships at John Brown University

"*Real Life Love* should be the new guidebook for anyone who falls short in their relationships. In a simple, relatable, and practical way, Michael Gibson takes readers on a journey to discover what deep, vibrant relationships look like. Read this book, and learn to love like never before."

—Alli Worthington, author of *Fierce Faith* and *Breaking Busy*

"We should all see our relationships as something that is highly treasured. Michael Gibson shows us how in this beautiful and special book."

—Tommy Barnett, senior pastor of Dream City Church and founder of the Los Angeles Dream Center

"Michael Gibson is an outstanding young man with an unmatched reputation. In his book, *Real Life Love,* he intertwines the practical advice from his late grandfather and his own easy-to-follow stories to create a must-read for anyone needing help with navigating emotions in all relationships, big and small. This book will leave a lasting impression on the reader and equip them with the necessary tools to make relationships the best they can be."

—Joe White, president of Kanakuk Kamps

"How different would your relationships be if you had spent your lifetime listening to the wisdom of Gary Smalley? Well, Michael Gibson has had that privilege of listening to his grandpa Gary, throughout his life. In this wonderful book, Michael shares Gary's wisdom and revelations on the very issues that either destroy or create fulfilling relationships—depending on how they are dealt with. And Michael does it all with the same warmth and humor that made Gary so beloved by his readers and audiences."

—Steven K. Scott, bestselling author of *Jesus Speaks* and *The Richest Man Who Ever Lived*

"Michael Gibson comes from a legacy that taught him love is a decision and that great relationships don't just happen. These lessons shine through on every page. He shares what was passed on to him in seven practical steps to great relationships. You won't be disappointed."

—Ted Cunningham, senior pastor of Woodland Hills Family Church and author of *Fun Loving You*

Real Life Love

SAYING GOODBYE
TO THE FAIRYTALE AND HELLO
TO TRUE RELATIONSHIPS

By

MICHAEL GIBSON

Foreword by
DR. LES PARROTT

Faith Words

New York   Nashville

Copyright © 2019 by Michael Gibson
Foreword copyright © 2019 by Dr. Les Parrott

Cover copyright © 2019 by Hachette Book Group, Inc.

FaithWords
Hachette Book Group
1290 Avenue of the Americas, New York, NY 10104
faithwords.com
twitter.com/faithwords

First Edition: August 2019

FaithWords is a division of Hachette Book Group, Inc. The FaithWords name and logo are trademarks of Hachette Book Group, Inc.

The publisher is not responsible for websites (or their content) that are not owned by the publisher.

Library of Congress Cataloging-in-Publication Data has been applied for.

ISBNs: 978-1-5460-0990-0 (trade paperback), 978-1-5460-0991-7 (ebook)

Printed in the United States of America

LSC-C

10 9 8 7 6 5 4 3 2 1

CONTENTS

PART 3
Growing in Love for Others

FOREWORD

I've got a question for you. It's simple, and you might be tempted to answer it quickly or flippantly. But I'd like you to give it some thought. Wait a couple beats before you answer. Here's the question: *What makes people happy?*

If you said being successful, you're not alone. Wealthy? You'll get plenty to agree with you. Playing video games or going to the movies? Sure. How about being popular or good looking? All of these are common responses. But as a psychologist and social scientist, let me tell you what we know for sure. The number-one clear winner—when it comes to making any of us truly happy—is *relationships*. Close ones.

It's not even a contest. Loving relationships are by far the most important factor in our personal well-being. Our happiness and joy are in direct correlation to the love we feel in our relationships. Why? For one reason, it is only in the context of connection with others that our deepest needs can be met. Whether we like it or not, each of us has an unshakable dependence on others. It's what philosopher

John Donne was getting at when he said so succinctly, "No man is an island." We need camaraderie, affection, friendship, and love. These are not options in life or sentimental trimmings. They are part of our species' survival kit. We *need* to belong. We need real life love.

That's why I'm grateful to my friend Michael Gibson for writing this incredibly helpful book. Before I knew Michael, I knew his grandfather Gary Smalley. As you may know, Gary was one of the most popular relationship experts ever. Whether it was on television, through his numerous bestselling books, or in sold-out arenas where he was speaking, people around the world loved Gary and his teachings on relationships. And I had the opportunity to share the stage with Gary on occasion. We got to know each other well. In fact, he became a mentor and friend. When I got the news that Gary had gone to heaven in 2016, I knew that I'd not only lost my friend, but I also knew that the world had lost a one-of-a-kind champion for real life love.

But here's something else I knew: For years, this renowned relationship expert had been grooming an apprentice, a novice who was soaking up his messages. Gary was pouring all of his priceless wisdom and treasured insights into his grandson Michael. In fact, for years it was Michael who traveled with Gary to assist him in his speaking engagements around the world. Michael was right there, just offstage or sitting in the audience, listening with teachable ears at every turn. Gary used to joke with me that Michael could speak about relationships as intelligently and with as much insight as he could.

So when Michael told me that he had boiled down Gary's relationship teachings into seven practical principles, he immediately had my attention. We've talked for countless hours together about the value his grandfather added to the lives of millions. And nobody on the planet has internalized Gary's messages more than Michael. That's why I'm thrilled he has put them into this book to share with you.

You've probably never met Michael, but if you did, you would love him. He's instantly accessible and authentic. He's got an easy laugh and a huge heart. He's loyal, dedicated, and smart. He's pretty much everything you'd want in a good friend. Oh, and he's passionate about teaching others what he has learned from his grandpa.

While your paths may never cross in person with Michael, you're going to feel like he's your friend after reading this book. *Real Life Love* is going to lift your vision for every relationship you have and give you practical steps for realizing healthier and more loving relationships on every front. You're going to be so happy that you read this book.

—Les Parrott, PhD
Founder of the Yada Assessment
and #1 *New York Times* bestselling author of
Saving Your Marriage Before It Starts

For my grandfathers

Love as Real as a Tiger

*…Love in its natural habitat. Love with its cage
wide open and ready to be experienced.*

Whether you like it or not, you currently star in a classic love story that has defined who you are. It's a crazy thought. In your love story, there are supporting characters and antagonists. Kings and queens. Knights, princesses, and villains. It's a timeless story that's been told countless times over the centuries.

I'm sure some of you are thinking: *But I've never even been in a relationship. How can this be possible?*

The surprising truth is that you don't have to be involved in a romantic relationship to be part of a love story. At the moment we came into this world, our love story began. For some, your story line is like your classic Disney movie: great parents, comfortable life, hardly any tough moments. You met (or will meet) Prince Charming or Cinderella and get married. And your love story becomes your kid's love story. You've been a part of generational love.

Or maybe your story looks more like the original Brothers Grimm fairytales. Stories in which good doesn't always prevail. Stories in which the villain always wins one way or another. Instead of growing up in love, you grew up in the castle on the other side of the tracks. Your parents gave up on you. Or they didn't seem to care if you succeeded or failed. You met what seemed to be Cinderella, but she just ended up being closer to the Wicked Witch of the West, emasculating and defeating. Or instead of Prince Charming, maybe he was Jafar from *Aladdin*. Suave on the outside. Dark and twisted on the inside. And you've found this to be true over and over.

While I know that every love story is different, I'm blessed to have grown up in a family that was greater than a Disney classic. And it was through my family life that I discovered the secrets to love at the tender age of ten. The secrets that men and women search for all their lives. The secrets that have inspired poems, Greek tragedies, Shakespearian plays, and Hollywood blockbuster movies.

Now, before you resent that statement and gather your pitchforks and villagers to form an angry mob, let me give some more context. No, it wasn't that the archangel Michael came down from heaven and whispered these secrets in my ear. And no, I didn't uncover some lost tablet written by Moses or Elijah from biblical times. These secrets came to me by way of my mentor, one of my biggest influences and also my best friend. His name was Gary Smalley.

Gary was my grandfather and also a world-renowned

marriage expert. When I was ten, he gave me an ultimatum. It happened one day after I'd had yet another argument with my mom. I literally ran to his house, which sounds more impressive than it really was. We were actually next-door neighbors.

I flew through his front door and found him typing something, probably his latest book on marriage and family at the time. I plopped down in his big armchair and started sharing what was on my heart: that my mom and I had another argument about my cleaning abilities (or lack thereof), and that I couldn't take it anymore. I was officially moving out, and into his upstairs bedroom.

My grandpa just smiled and asked me if I would like to discover a way to end all arguments with my mom. And not just that, but live in harmony with my siblings, friends, family members, and even strangers for the rest of my life. He asked me if I wanted to learn to love for real. It was there, sitting on a La-Z-Boy chair in my grandpa's study, that I learned the secrets to loving well. The secrets worth a thousand suns. The secrets to wholehearted, vibrant, committed, ride-or-die relationships. And honestly, I didn't realize what I had until I became much older.

WHAT'S LOVE GOT TO DO WITH IT?

Love is such an elusive word. It can mean so many different things. Love can mean the genuine affection you have for cookie dough ice cream or Chinese food. Or maybe the

favorite place you "love" to sit in church. Or that sweater
that you "love" to slip on during a cold, wintry day. It blows
my mind that in the English language we use that same
word to describe our most meaningful relationships too.

I use *love* to describe the way I feel about my mom,
whose unrelenting and unwavering encouragement got
me through my darkest of days. Or my dad, who worked
hard my entire life (and still does) to put food on the table
and give my sisters and me the best shot in life we could
possibly have.

It's the same word I used to say goodbye to my grandfather when he passed away on March 6, 2016. And it's the
same word I'll say someday to my bride as we rock back
and forth on the front porch of our future home as two old
people, watching the sun set on our golden years and the
life we built together.

That little four-letter word has many identities. If it were
a person, it would probably have a case of multiple personality disorder. When you think of the word *love*, you probably automatically think of the most well-known face love
wears, which the Greeks called *eros*. This word literally
means "sexual love." C. S. Lewis, in his book *The Four Loves*,
describes *eros* as "being in love." Or "that kind of love which
lovers are 'in.'" While, yes, this is a legitimate personality
of love, and one that creates those "butterflies" when we
start a new relationship, that's not the only face love wears.

Love can also be identified with another word the
Greeks used: *philia*, the type of love friends share. In fact,

it literally means having a genuine fondness and a friendly regard toward someone. While this type of love is good for lunching with your best friend on Tuesdays or giving your work buddy a friendly fist bump in passing, that's really the extent of these relationships. *Philia* exists in the root of society. It's a neighbor-helping-neighbor type of love. Nothing deep. Just a pat on the back, or a smile in passing.

The love I'm talking about is not *eros* or *philia*. It's not some Hollywood, hot-pink, roman-candle, Leonardo-DiCaprio-raising-a-glass-of-champagne-with-fireworks-exploding-behind-him type of love. It's not the secret to attracting the opposite sex in such a manner that they fall into your arms just from looking at you. Nor is it a way to get the phone number of every eligible bachelor or bachelorette you come across, or a love that is no deeper than the casual "Hi, how are you" at church. If you think that's what this book is about, then I would encourage you to keep reading. Because while those types of relationships are pleasurable or comfortable at the time, they're about as deep as a puddle.

These superficial "loves" will tear your marriage apart, keep your parents at arm's length, and produce friends who are only cool to party with on the weekends. While these loves will satisfy you temporarily, they'll leave you feeling like you're missing something, like there's something more. Something that life is hiding away. If you're chasing *eros* and *philia* loves, after a while you're going to wonder why your relationships have no meaning. And you'll find yourself wishing for relationships that are deeper than the world's oceans and as strong as an ox and that have zero blind spots. You're going to desire a love that's as true as this book you're holding in your hands or listening to on your earphones.

The love I'm talking about is the kind of love the Greeks called *agape*. The Apostle Paul describes *agape* love so beautifully in his letter to the early church in Corinth. But before he told them about it, Paul made sure his readers knew how important loving this way is. It turns out that without this type of love, we'll never be able to be effective in what we do.

If I speak with human eloquence and angelic ecstasy but don't love, I'm nothing but the creaking of a rusty gate. If I speak God's Word with power, revealing all his mysteries and making everything plain as day, and if I have faith that says to a mountain, "Jump," and it jumps, but I don't love, I'm nothing. (1 Corinthians 13:1–2)

So what is this type of love? What is this love Paul so fervently believes we need? Luckily, he answers this for us in the very next passage:

...Love never gives up. Love cares more for others than for self. Love doesn't want what it doesn't have. Love doesn't strut, doesn't have a swelled head, doesn't force itself on others, isn't always "me first," doesn't fly off the handle, doesn't keep score of the sins of others, doesn't revel when others grovel, takes pleasure in the flowering of truth, puts up with anything, trusts God always, always looks for the best, never looks back, but keeps going to the end. (1 Corinthians 13:4–7)

That is the type of love we're focusing on. The kind of love that fills your soul with the light of a thousand sunrises. The kind of love that makes the twists and turns of life worthwhile. That, my friends, is real life love.

IS IT POSSIBLE?

That kind of love seems a little far out there, doesn't it? I'm sure you're thinking, *Wow, Michael, this is great and all, but that's just not possible.* But is it? Part of my discovery process of understanding love and how to do it well came during a meeting with world-renowned neuroscientist Dr. Caroline Leaf. To give her the proper introduction she deserves, Dr. Leaf has dedicated her life and research to answering one question: What is the brain's primary purpose? Her work has been groundbreaking for researchers trying to learn more about the way we think.

During our meeting in Scottsdale, Arizona, Dr. Leaf told our group that the brain is designed to do just one thing. This one thing becomes the essence of who we are as humans and is vital to our survival. Can you guess what it is? If you guessed it's to get food and shelter like I did, you're wrong. It's to love.

No wonder the Apostle Paul ends his letter in 1 Corinthians 13 with these words: "Three things will last forever—faith, hope, and love—and the greatest of these is love" (1 Cor. 13:13 NLT). You are literally designed for this type of love. Love sustains our well-being, nurtures our minds, and gives us the strength to keep pressing on!

So if we are literally made to love, then don't you think we're destined for the love Paul outlines in 1 Corinthians 13? You bet. We are on this earth to have great relationships. To give love and receive love with open arms. Relationships might be one of the greatest gifts (outside of salvation) that God gave us. And I'm not referring to just your relationship with your spouse or significant other. We engage in so many different relationships each and every day. When your mom calls you on your way to work, that's engaging in a relationship. Smiling and saying hi in passing to the guy at your workplace who seems a little rough around the edges—that's being in a relationship. Life is relationships, and the rest is just details. So if life truly is relationships, then shouldn't we put mastering how to love on the top of our to-do list?

LET'S TALK FOR REAL

So many of us put relationships on the bottom shelf. Like that old battleship replica you thought you'd build in your spare time, it just sits there, collecting dust and never realizing its full potential. It's tempting to invest all of our time in creating wealth, climbing the corporate ladder, and "making" something of ourselves. Or it's easy to imagine the perfect fairytale love story. You see your wedding, getting married, going on a honeymoon, buying a house, getting a dog, cooking dinners, traveling around the world, having all the money you need, and finally living your happily ever after. No room in this story for conflict. No room for difficult times. Just smooth sailing and long walks on the beach. Sounds nice, doesn't it?

Well, let me press stop on that mental movie that looks and sounds like something straight from the Hallmark Channel. If that's the way you see your life and relationships panning out, then you are in for a wake-up call. In that "perfect" scenario I just mentioned, I conveniently left out the parts about the hours that go into planning that wedding, the time you spend working through the issues you and your future spouse both carry, dealing with the change of living with someone new, the spontaneous pregnancy that comes out of nowhere, your new puppy that pees constantly around the house, the rising cost of groceries, the fear of losing your job from all those missed days "seeing the world," the sudden expense of fixing your broken transmission in that car you've had since high school.

Those are two very different scenes, aren't they? One paints a beautiful picture, the other just pulls back the curtain to reveal the 360-degree view. Life is complicated. And can you imagine how all of those things take a toll on our relationships?

While there's nothing wrong with wanting to provide for yourself or family, or with envisioning the best for your future, that's just the tip of the iceberg of what life has to offer. I believe that true happiness and joy are rooted in our relationships. If your relationships are healthy, that means the roots of your life are capable of producing a tall, strong tree. On the other hand, if your relationships are in shambles and you never fully grasp how to truly love for real, your roots will wither and your tree might sprout just a few inches out of the ground before dying from the harsh conditions life has to offer.

LOVE AS REAL AS A TIGER

You might be wondering what gives me the authority to take on such a Goliath of a topic. I mean, there aren't any letters in front of my name or behind it. If you looked at my bio, chances are you noticed that I don't pastor a megachurch. I didn't graduate from Harvard Divinity School as a master theologian. I'm not Dr. Gibson. In fact, I failed psychology my freshman year of college. I'm not writing as a master of love who knows all the secrets to happy relationships. Instead, I'm writing as a fellow struggler just like you. A struggler who has failed over and over in relationships. A struggler who, at the writing of this book, isn't even married yet. A struggler who also thought at one time that my relationships were going to be awesome no matter what I did.

That's why I wrote this book. To share what I've been learning. To share what has worked for me and what hasn't. To pass on the wisdom given to me by my grandfather, which I have tested and implemented in my life. It's time we learn how to love for real.

During the writing of this book, I was often asked why I chose to write about relationships for my first book. These friends wondered why, right out of the gate, I chose to speak on this topic of love. And I'm sure you might be wondering about the answer to that one too. I mean, after all, there are a lot of other things to focus on.

But you see, I don't think there is a more important topic to spend our precious time working on than relationships. That's why I started here. Because I've seen firsthand how healthy relationships have the incredible power to take someone to new heights. Good relationships move you into more. More love. More intimacy. Less stress. Greater success. And an overall better outlook on life.

During the past few years, I've been discovering what works. Like a scientist, I've been testing and trying the various love skills I learned from my grandfather and family. I was taught that love works when it's working right. But how do we know what works? Just like Liam Neeson in the movie *Taken*, we need a particular set of skills in order to succeed at something. And this book is going to let you in on what I've discovered to be the most effective means of creating real love in any relationship. Throughout this book, I'm going to give you seven principles that I've found most effective in my pursuit of real life love:

Principle #1: *Honor.* You highly honor everyone in your life.

Principle #2: *Anger.* You keep your anger levels low.

Principle #3: *Forgiveness.* You find every way possible to forgive.

Principle #4: *Celebrating Trials.* You take personal responsibility for finding God's blessing in every trial.

Principle #5: *Memorizing God's Word.* You learn and understand the teachings of Jesus.

Principle #6: *Servanthood.* You lay down your life as a servant.

Principle #7: *Understanding Personality.* You discover and understand the way people tick.

When my little sister Zoie was four years old, I took her on a "French-fry date," just the two of us. We sat together at McDonald's and ate our French fries (her favorite food) with pure delight. I told her that she could pick anything she could possibly imagine to do on our date. So with a big smile, she said that she wanted to go see the tigers. Luckily, I knew where we could find some.

To a four-year-old, the city zoo is a place of wonder and amazement (and for some adults too, me included). Suddenly, you come face-to-face with the creatures and animals you only read about in picture books or see on television. And what a glorious moment that is.

From the moment we walked through the gates of the

zoo, Zoie's eyes got as big as saucers. She looked around in sheer delight and wonder at the monkeys dancing in their cages, the tropical birds singing tunes in sync, the elephants parading around with authority, and, of course, the tigers. As they paced back and forth, their orange bodies and black stripes mystified my little sister.

After staring at the pacing tigers behind the glass, she looked up at me and asked if the tiger was "real life." It hit me: *She probably thinks this glass is just a giant television screen and that she's just watching a video.* I told her that those tigers were as real life as she and I were. And that if that glass wasn't there to protect us, we'd be in trouble. But she still didn't believe me.

Luckily, we got the chance of a lifetime. One observant zookeeper noticed my sister's infatuation and asked if we wanted to watch the feeding crew give the giant cats their lunch. The zookeeper led us behind the cage and into a back area where the tigers were fed their meals. Zoie and I watched as they opened the slit in the tigers' cages and slid in their food. The giant cats devoured their lunch with loud chomps.

"I've always wanted to see a tiger in real life," Zoie said, fascinated.

How would you like to see love in real life? Are you ready to get behind the glass and experience true, real love for yourself? No fairytales, no singing characters or lovable animal sidekicks. No three-step, five-step, or ten-step programs. And no three easy payments of $39.99. Just love in its natural habitat. Love with its cage wide open and ready to be experienced.

Before you turn the page, I have just one question. And it's the same question my grandpa asked me all those years ago:

Are you ready to learn to love for real?

PART 1

Growing in Love for Yourself

CHAPTER 1

Honor

The beating heart of our relationships is honor.
Without honor, real life love cannot take place.

There really isn't a more exciting thrill for me than panning for gold. I love the idea of pouring a mound of uninteresting dirt and rock into a sifter and running it through a stream of flowing water to see if, just by a small chance, I'll find something extraordinary in the midst of ordinary mud.

The first time I ever panned for gold was at a theme park in Branson, Missouri, called Silver Dollar City. While everyone else in our group was running from rollercoaster to rollercoaster and pounding down the funnel cakes, I was camped out at the gold panning station. The park sold these individual bags of dirt for $9.99, which was a small price to pay for the chance of finding a giant gold nugget in your sifter.

After carefully selecting my bag of dirt, I took it over

to the sifting station, where I poured my newly purchased dirt onto a sifter, which looked a bit like a window screen. I then shook my sifter back and forth in a trough through a stream of flowing water. Then I removed my sifter and carefully inspected it to see if there was any gold.

I probably went through five bags of dirt that day, and I did in fact find gold. Each bag contained a few small, shiny gold flakes, which still sit in my desk drawer today. The employee managing the gold panning station delicately picked out each flake of gold and sealed them all in a small glass vial with clear water. That way, I could forever treasure my discoveries.

Gold has forever captivated the hearts of man. Homer wrote about it in his works *The Iliad* and *The Odyssey*, making mention of gold as the glory of the immortals and a sign of wealth among ordinary humans. The ancient Incas used to refer to this precious metal as "tears of the sun." Even the Bible mentions gold. In Genesis 2:10–12, the author talks about a river that flowed out of the Garden of Eden and "into the land of Havilah, where there is gold. And the gold of that land is good" (Gen. 2:11–12 ESV).

I'm sure you're wondering how a mineral that has a shiny and shimmering yellow appearance could be so valuable. Why not copper or iron? What's so special about gold? No one really knows the beginnings of why gold has held such a special place in society since literally the earliest records of our history. But I have a theory. One day someone took a fresh look at this unique mineral and saw rare beauty. As people began to see its value, these bits of earth were elevated to a place of high worth. This same principle of value applies to each person in your life. And that principle is called *honor*.

WHAT IS HONOR?

The beating heart of our relationships is honor. Without honor, real life love cannot take place. To illustrate what exactly honor is, let's go back to the example of gold. Imagine I offered you a solid brick of gold. What would you do? Would you refuse it? Or would you just throw it outside like an ordinary red clay brick? Of course not! You would probably immediately accept the gift, thank me over and over for giving it to you, and regularly maintain and take care of it so it holds its worth. And you would guard it. Probably by keeping it in a thick metal safe, away from thieves.

Practicing honor in your relationships is as simple as treating people like you would that priceless gold brick—with exceedingly high worth and value. Honor, according to *Merriam-Webster's Dictionary*, is "respect that is given to someone who is admired—one whose worth brings respect or fame."

The first step in learning to practice honor is to really get to know *why* you truly love that person. If you think about it, each of us is an individual bag of dirt, just waiting to be sifted through, our unique qualities waiting to be discovered like little flakes of priceless gold. Relationships are really the panning experience. God has placed people in your life, maybe a significant other, parents, brothers, sisters, or friends, as an opportunity to look past the "dirt" and see how God sees us—as having tremendously high worth.

As you begin to grow deeper in your relationships with people, one way of approaching this concept of honor is to simply agree with God: Value what He values. He loves us more than our minds can possibly comprehend. Imagine your relationships through God's eyes. How much more would you love your family and friends if you saw them as God sees them? I believe that's truly the "secret sauce" to harmony in all your relationships: to discover the unique high value within each person you know.

When you make the decision to value people like God does, it's like He opens your heart and does open heart surgery on the way you love. Suddenly, you're more open to the beautiful treasures around you. The things that normally would drive you crazy and cause a big argument are suddenly almost endearing. You'll find you're more loving, patient, kind, joyful, and compassionate. Real love follows honor. When you honor someone, or highly value their unique qualities and personality traits, love flows like a roaring river. But it starts with the value that we place upon people (not the other way around). The way you feel about someone is determined by how much you value them.

Remember when Kim Kardashian was married to NBA

player Kris Humphries for seventy-two days? I remember watching the very episode of their reality show when Kim makes the decision to leave Kris. In a nutshell, through the tears and sobs, Kim says she needs to leave because she isn't happy and thus the love isn't there.

Here's the truth of the matter—love exists only where there is honor.

Kim probably could have saved a lot of time, money, and embarrassment if she had begun to see Kris's special and unique, and at times quirky, qualities as highly valuable and worthy of celebration. Instead of seeing them as annoying, frustrating, or childlike, what if Kim had seen them how God sees them? What if she was able to see them like golden nuggets that were worth more than all the Cartier bracelets in the world? Who knows, there might even have been a North Humphries, instead of a North West, walking the earth today.

HONORING YOURSELF

So, how do we begin this quest to honor others? The first step is to choose to honor yourself. If you can't honor yourself, then how are you going to be able to honor others? I believe that a lack of honor is one of the root causes of the evil we see in today's society. People who don't honor themselves as God's beloved are more likely to treat themselves poorly and, in turn, hurt others. My family coined a phrase that my siblings and I used to say over and over: "Honor

God, others, and His *creation*." We are part of God's creation. God doesn't need to sift through our dirt to find our
unique and special qualities. He finds them immediately,
with pinpoint accuracy. God has an honor list a mile long
for you and sees you as his most valuable possession.

We all need reminders of this truth, because God's love
for us is the foundation of honor. Jesus told us to love others
as we love *ourselves*. Think about that! Understanding our
own value to God is essential.

Just as it is unwise to build your house on sand, it is
hard to build a foundation of honor in your relationships
and truly experience real life love if you don't honor and
love yourself. You are worth more to God than all the gold
in the world. God loves you, and He loves me. Faults and
weaknesses and all. So let's accept the value God has chosen to place on us. If we can do that, we can begin to see the
value in other people and join with God in lifting them up.

WHAT CAN I DO?

But at this point you might be asking yourself, *How is this
possible?* or *How am I supposed to honor someone when I'm so
angry and disappointed with them?* The reality is that honor
recognizes that everyone has faults, blind spots, and "logs
in their eyes" (Matt. 7:4 NLT). This includes you and me!
We all have our flaws. They're what makes us unique. But
they don't make us any less valuable. When you begin to

see relationships as a means to discover the unique value of each person—instead of as something whose sole purpose is to make you happy—real life love begins to blossom. That's where the greatest joy and happiness in your relationships comes from. You get to be the panner, sifting through the dirt and mud and discovering the unique traits that make up the people you love. But it all comes down to a decision.

A great first step toward making the decision to honor, to intentionally look at the unique qualities in people as Jesus sees them, is making an honor list. It's super simple! Just think of someone you love, or even someone you can't stand. Then think of only their best qualities and jot down some of the things that come to mind. Yes, this can be hard. And might even take some time. But believe me, it will change your outlook on the person. Especially when you're in a tough spot.

You can even try making an honor list for yourself. What do you value about yourself? What are some of your positive qualities? Learn what makes you unique, and what makes you tick. Remember, you are a rare gold brick! The rarest of rare! Then jot down on paper or on a device of your choice everything that comes to mind. Make it your phone's background image and look at it every day. Understanding what it means to honor begins with looking at yourself. And by building that solid foundation of honoring yourself, you build your house on solid rock.

My friend and mentor Dr. Les Parrott taught a class

called Relationships 101 at Seattle Pacific University in Seattle, Washington, for thirty years. On the very first day of each semester, he would ask his students to write down this profound truth: "If you try to build intimacy with another person before you've done the difficult work of getting whole, all your relationships become an attempt to complete yourself."

Les would remind his students that their relationships could be only as healthy as they were. Many times, I have seen friends jump into relationships, even going as far as marrying the person, because they believe it will make life better or that being married would end all of their problems. If you want to get married for the sole reason that it will make your life more pleasurable (with constant affection, sex, and attention), then let me burst that bubble for you. It just isn't true. Your relationships will fall flat each and every time. Today is the day to get yourself emotionally healthy, before making that sacred commitment. And if you're reading this book as a married person, it's never too late to begin this journey. Your spouse and family will thank you forever for taking on this challenge.

A SPICY SITUATION

For some reason, it was always easier for me to keep a "hurt list" or "pain-in-the-neck list" about people. It stood out in my mind whenever I thought of anybody I had negative beliefs about. When I was in high school, I had a Spanish teacher who couldn't have been more mean. She was constantly embarrassing me in front of my peers. Foreign language was always hard for me. Like algebra, Spanish was a class I dreaded each day. And it seemed that every time I had forgotten to study the previous night or practice my vocabulary list, my teacher made a point of ridiculing me.

One day my worst nightmare was realized: a verbal pop quiz. I'm sure you could have literally seen the fear in my eyes. I wasn't prepared. As panic overtook my body, I wanted the earth to open up so I could escape and hide. Guess who she called on first? Question after question, I didn't get one answer right. She then proceeded to make an example out of me of what not to do in Spanish class. I was so embarrassed.

So I took it upon myself to be a martyr. I was out to save my fellow classmates and any students after me from her wrath. Immediately after class and fuming with anger, I marched into the principal's office. Determined to get this woman fired, I began to share with my school's principal all of the "horrible" things this woman had done to me, one thing after the next, hoping my principal would take my side and invite me to do the honors of firing her myself!

Her response was a bit different from what I expected. My principal said very gently, "Michael, I think you need to take an extra-long lunch break. Why don't you go get something to eat and we can talk later?" After walking out of her office, I checked my phone and noticed I had a text from my grandpa inviting me to join him for lunch at our favorite Mexican place down the road from my high school. *How ironic*, I thought to myself. I got in my car and drove the short distance to the restaurant. The whole drive I was practicing my best *Celebrity Apprentice*–style "You're fired," which I was planning to use on my Spanish teacher when I returned to school.

Once we were seated, my grandpa asked me how my day was going. I proceeded to share with him the same words I used with my principal. I went on and on about how terrible this teacher was, how she embarrassed me in front of all my peers, and how I would dethrone her. I told him that it was now my new life mission to get her fired before I graduated. Grandpa then got really serious. He looked me in the eyes and said, "You've shared all the bad things about this teacher, but what about the good things?"

After almost choking on my chicken enchilada, I looked at him, dazed and confused.

"The good? Grandpa, did you not just hear what I said? This woman is Satan himself disguised as a Spanish teacher. Are you crazy?" I said.

He wasn't crazy. He was dead serious. Grandpa had me ask our waiter for a pen and an extra napkin (in Spanish of course) and advised me to practice honor by writing down anything and everything that was positive about my teacher. It wasn't easy. But after several items on the list, I realized that maybe the reason she was so hard on me was the potential I had as a Spanish student. Or as a student in general. Maybe she saw something inside me that I didn't. Maybe she wasn't evil after all. Here are a few points from my list:

- **Driven:** She challenges me on a daily basis to be my best.
- **Passionate:** She loves the Spanish language and is eager to teach her students this beautiful language.
- **Talented:** Being the chair of the foreign language department, she is extremely knowledgeable of foreign languages and cultures. Especially Spanish.
- **Caring:** She wants to see me do well in Spanish and is pushing me to commit to excelling in her class.

All of a sudden, I started to feel icky inside. All of the words I spewed to my principal about this woman made me feel sick. It wasn't until after making my honor list that I realized what I had done.

"I think you need to seek forgiveness from your principal," my grandpa said.

He was right. Once we paid the check, I raced back to school and made a beeline directly for the principal's office. I knocked on the door and entered. I could tell she was bracing for another blowout. After seeking her forgiveness, I realized that it was time for me to in turn forgive my teacher.

Of course, Spanish class didn't get any easier. The lectures still came, the embarrassment still occurred, my terrible pronunciation was still prevalent. But each time something embarrassing happened, I would reach into my backpack and feel the soft paper napkin, which held my honor list for her. Each time, it reminded me that my teacher was to be honored like a priceless gold brick, because that's how Jesus sees her. And later I found my anger turning to understanding and compassion.

HONORING FOR REAL

A few months later, as the school year was coming to a close, my teacher announced she was retiring. As a gift, I gave her my napkin of the things I honored about her. Big tears filled her eyes. She said it was the nicest thing a student had ever done for her. Though today I can barely remember the Spanish word for "hello," I am still reminded of that story and how God first taught me to honor by focusing on the positive qualities of people.

I love these words from Jesus: "Where your treasure is, your heart will be also" (Matt. 6:21 NIV). Affection for your significant other, family, friends, and someday your spouse will continue to grow as you maintain an awareness of each person as a treasure highly valued by God. But it's also important to remember that love is a decision. I had to make the decision to make the list about my teacher. It's also important to keep it in front of you and add to it as often as you can. Even though the embarrassment in class hurt in the moment, I couldn't wait to refer back to my list. I even added to it a few times! When you invest time, energy, words, and actions in treasuring someone this way, your heart will grow in love for them.

My friend Rob is the ultimate example of loving this way. Our friendship dates back to high school, and I always marveled at his unique brand of love, one that was way beyond his years. Rob is one of those people who truly understands how to love people. From the popular jocks to the lonely, misconstrued, and outcast, there wasn't anyone who wasn't a friend of Rob's in high school. And he never had anything unkind to say about anyone. Rob had a gift for connecting with everybody. Especially the people who didn't get loved all that often. The quirky kids, the down-and-outers, the kids who were rough around the edges. It didn't matter to Rob. He always included them in his social circles and sat by them at lunch. Everyone loved Rob, and he truly demonstrated love too.

Rob and I got the chance to reconnect on a recent trip to Israel. While we caught up on our lives, we walked down the Via Dolorosa, the road Jesus took when He carried the Cross to Calvary. As we walked along the old and ancient cobblestoned roads among the winding streets of Jerusalem, Rob recalled a conversation we'd had in high school while walking the hills of Branson Hills Golf Club (we played on the high school golf team together). He told me I shared then that I hoped to write a book one day.

That reminder struck me, because while I had confided that particular dream to a few people in high school, their response was usually laughter and comments like "Yeah right, and one day I'll be the president of the United States." But not Rob. He told me as we walked the course that day, he thought I'd be a published author and that I ought to pursue my dream. He didn't know that as I was walking those old and sacred roads in Jerusalem with him,

I was dreaming up this book you're holding in your hands right now.

With this very concept in mind, I was curious as to how he was able to love everyone and anyone, no matter if they were the most popular or the most reclusive. How was he able to see my uniqueness when no one else could? Rob's answer was something I'll never forget.

He said that he always tries his best to see people for who they are to Christ. He searches and treasure hunts for the unique and special qualities that make people remarkable and takes into consideration how deeply loved and honored those special quirks are by Jesus. Though some qualities may seem different and weird to everyone else, once you look past the thin human veil and see the riches that the Father sees, it's easy to love people for real. In fact, our affection even grows for them as we understand how valuable they are. All we have to do is make the decision to see people in this way. It's a choice!

AN HONORING QUESTION

Abandonment is one of the deepest relational wounds of the millennial generation. If you are reading this book and were born between the years of 1983 and 2000, chances are you've experienced or been touched by abandonment from a family member. Maybe your mom or dad left. Or you've seen your friends struggle with this. In fact, according to

the American Psychological Association, between 40 percent and 50 percent of marriages in the United States will
end in divorce, a statistic that has been looming over Amer-
icans for the past two decades. This means there's a fifty-
fifty chance that you, the reader, come from a divorced
family.

We are living in a time when the sanctity of marriage
hangs on by a thread. People assume that marriage equals
happiness. And if there ever comes a time when "happy" is
no longer part of that equation, then the divorce papers are
signed. But how is that an example of honor? Honor says,
"I love you, even through your imperfections." We can't
abandon our relationships just because we go through hard
times. This is true for every relationship.

My mom and I are a lot alike. We have very similar personalities. So we tend to be the ones in the family who dis-
agree the most. We've gone through some rough times. I
like to say that we must have some Italian blood flowing
through our veins, because we've been involved in some
pretty heated arguments. But here's the difference: I'm not
walking out on my relationship with my mom because we
fight or go through hard times. She's my mom, and always
will be. End of story.

But so many people have the tendency to throw in the
towel and say goodbye to what could potentially be a time
of growing together and coming out on the other side with
a strengthened relationship. This is why I want to challenge you to be different from the status quo. It's time, as

a generation that is plagued with relationship wounds and hurts, not to give up—and to honor through the tough times.

By the way, I want to be clear: If you are in an abusive relationship—with a significant other, spouse, parent, friend, or even boss—I'm not saying that you should stay in it. You need to remove yourself from that circumstance (which takes a lot of strength and bravery in itself). The relationships I'm referring to are healthy but just going through a dry patch.

If you're wondering how to stay committed and engaged in your relationship, and accepting my challenge not to walk out, just take a page from Jesus' playbook. I'm always amazed by the fact that Jesus sticks by our side no matter what. He chooses us, even when we wouldn't choose ourselves. He loves us when we feel unlovable. He doesn't abandon us when loving us gets hard. He chooses to keep pursuing a relationship with us, because He knows keeping us close will someday be worth it in His renewed kingdom. This is how we should see our relationships: as things that deserve our best shot to stay in, to stay engaged.

If you have trouble with this, here's a statement that will change everything if you believe it: "There is nothing you can do that can make me stop loving you."

My mom and dad would say that to me often when I was growing up. Talk about a powerful statement. To test its sincerity, I'd say things like, "Well, what if I go to prison?" They would kindly respond, "No, if you go to prison, we will visit you and bring you cakes, and we'll never stop loving you. We're your parents. We are who we are, and we will never stop loving you, no matter what you do. You can reject us. Pull away from anything we believe. It doesn't matter what you do; we'll always love you, and we'll be there if you need us."

When my parents said that to me, I couldn't help but feel loved. And it helped train me to understand that no matter how desperate any relationship gets, it's always worth fighting for. Real life love doesn't give up when things get difficult. It sticks it out. And works hard to achieve harmony. Real life love is all about second chances, and never strikes out. Are you willing to start having similar conversations in your relationships?

THE CLIMB

Recently, I was visiting some newly married friends in Colorado. Being married for just a few months, Ryan and Lindsay were deep in the honeymoon stage. All of the cute looks, pet names, and public displays of affection were starting to annoy me.

"Do you guys ever fight?" I asked them over dinner.

"Not a chance!" they said, gazing into each other's eyes.

Oh great, I thought. *This will be fun during our hike tomorrow.* I was visiting Colorado not only to see my friends but also to climb my first "fourteener," a term used for mountains at least 14,000 feet high. I just knew the entire day would be filled with lovey-dovey remarks.

When you climb a 14,000-foot mountain, it's not a basic stroll in the woods. It's serious business. That night we packed our backpacks and laid out our hiking shoes and the various warm layers we were planning on wearing during the hike. We packed a bunch of water, and even oxygen tanks because of the severe altitude change.

Our day began at two in the morning. You have to get an early start if you want to summit. Because Colorado is known for storms that can accumulate out of nowhere, it's important to take this safety precaution. So we gathered up our gear and piled into Ryan's SUV. Our mountain of choice was Mount Sherman, which was about a three-hour drive from their home in Colorado Springs.

The entire way was filled with more married-people conversation. As a single guy, I wasn't interested in the current mortgage rates for a home or the latest neighborhood news about their subdivision in the suburbs. I was interested in one thing and one thing only: climbing, summiting, and ultimately surviving Mount Sherman.

Our hike began in the dark, with headlamps guiding our path. Mount Sherman's elevation at the summit is 14,036 feet. So we had a long hike ahead of us. Each step was tougher than the last. I felt like I was breathing through a straw because of the thin air. My legs were like jelly. My motto for the day quickly turned into "Just One More Step." Over and over I said that phrase as we got closer and closer to the summit.

After we made it to the top, we snapped our photos and gazed at the breathtaking view. But it was now time to start our descent. And we needed to go down quickly: Ryan was starting to feel the symptoms of altitude sickness. Careful step after careful step we slowly inched our way down Mount Sherman. Exhausted, our feet covered with blisters, we finally made it back to the car all in one piece.

We didn't waste much time getting back into our car. Still woozy and sick from the altitude, Ryan reached for the handle of the passenger-side door just as Lindsay grabbed it.

"Babe, can you drive? I'm not sure I can stay awake for the drive home," Ryan said.

"Ryan, I am exhausted too. Can you just drive?" Lindsay replied.

"No, I really need to sit this one out. I think I might fall asleep at the wheel."

"Ugh! Can't you just suck it up?" Lindsay asked grumpily.

"Fine," Ryan grumbled as he climbed into the driver's side.

I climbed in and immediately drifted off to sleep as Ryan started driving down the tight mountain road. We had made it only a few miles when all of a sudden, I woke up to Lindsay screaming and the car swerving out of control toward an embankment. Ryan slammed on the brakes. He had fallen asleep at the wheel.

Luckily, Ryan woke up in time to stop the vehicle from pitching off the side of the cliff. Lindsay didn't know what had happened. Disoriented from also being half asleep, she yelled, "Ryan! You could have killed us! I can't believe you fell asleep at the wheel!"

"Babe, I told you I wasn't fit to drive," Ryan snapped. "I

have a splitting headache, and my stomach is sick. I told you I needed you to drive."

Ryan and Lindsay then began to engage in a full-blown argument. Going back and forth, they hurled sharp insults at each other.

"Remember in our vows, when you promised to obey me?" Ryan snapped.

"I'm sorry, I didn't realize I'm just one of your royal subjects, your highness!" Lindsay fired back. Unbeknownst to them, I wasn't asleep in the back seat. I was hearing every word.

After their royal argument subsided, the car was quieter than it had been the whole trip. Ryan was looking straight ahead; Lindsay was looking out the side window. All of a sudden, I heard Ryan say, "Lindsay, do you think we're really going to make it? Do you think we could ever fall out of love?"

Ryan and Lindsay come from two totally different upbringings. Lindsay is the daughter of pastors and grew up in a home where the word *divorce* was a curse word. Ryan, on the other hand, grew up in the foster-care system. His parents abandoned him when he was six years old. He found Jesus at Lindsay's parents' church when he was fourteen and was eventually adopted by a foster family.

Big tears flooded Lindsay's eyes. She later told me that her parents used to regularly watch my grandfather's marriage-education video series, *Hidden Keys to Loving Relationships*, when they were a young couple. Lindsay would often hear her dad say to her mom, "There is nothing you could do that could make me stop loving you. I love you forever and ever." Remembering this conversation, she turned to her husband and took his hand. "Ryan, the day I said 'I do' is the day I promised to love you forever," she said through tears. "There is nothing you could do and nothing you could say that could make me stop loving you."

Tears started streaming down Ryan's face too. No one had ever said that to him before. It looked like Lindsay had just handed him a million bucks. This important statement instantly summed up her feelings for Ryan. It took the awkward guessing out of the equation. Ryan later told me that he had never felt more loved. Lindsay valued Ryan like precious gold. It made him feel that no matter what, Lindsay was always going to love him. *"There is nothing that you can ever do that would cause me to stop loving you."*

CHAPTER 2

Anger

*Anger is our response to lies
we believe about ourselves.*

I'm a sucker for kids' movies. There's nothing like a great cartoon to transport my imagination back to its glory days. For two amazing hours, I feel like I'm reintroduced to the ten-year-old me. I giggle and cry just as I did back in the days when I thought there really was a SpongeBob SquarePants who lived in a pineapple under the sea.

In my opinion, the crème de la crème of kids' cartoon movies are made by the geniuses at Pixar Animation Studios. I don't know how they do it, but every film they make is magic. Everything is top-notch, from the characters to the story lines and, of course, their state-of-the-art motion graphics.

Of all the Pixar movies, my favorite is *Inside Out*. It's a masterpiece that goes inside the head of a twelve-year-old girl named Riley and tells the stories of the emotions that control the way she feels. The five core emotions we meet are Joy, Sadness, Anger, Disgust, and Fear.

Throughout the film, we see how Riley's family's move from a small, charming town in Minnesota to the hustle-and-bustle of San Francisco takes a toll on her emotions. She has a hard time adjusting to a new school and making new friends and she misses her life back in Minnesota. Even the pizza in San Francisco doesn't make the cut for Riley compared to her old town's.

These difficulties set her emotions on a journey to discover how to handle all of these changes. As her emotions try to understand how to deal with everything around her, Riley begins to withdraw from her family. Joy and Sadness are out of the picture, which leaves Anger, Disgust, and Fear at the helm. Each takes control of the way she is feeling. Her temper becomes sharp toward her mom and dad. She starts to feel anxiety about school. And she finds life downright disgusting. This leads to some disastrous results. Her emotions force an emotional shut down, and we see Riley make some pretty bad decisions. She's angry, alone, and depressed.

When I first saw this movie, I was reminded that we are in the midst of a pandemic circling the globe. There are millions of Rileys who wander through life feeling angry—they're closed off and hurt by someone or something. Dr. Don Colbert, a leading medical expert, says in his book *Deadly Emotions* that this disease can weaken your immune system and cause heart problems and premature aging. And its destructive symptoms don't stop at just medical ailments. It also has the ability to drive away the people you love and leave you in a cold and empty place.

You never hear about it in the news. It's not as well-known as other diseases like the Ebola virus or Zika. Yet millions of people around the world carry it. And it's what Riley suffers from during her low point in the movie.

The disease is called anger. And it's a silent killer. Many experience its symptoms every day and don't know why or how to treat it. I believe that anger is a leading contributor to most of the issues we face in our relationships. And it needs to stop. If you want to experience real life love and relationships that are true, you can't even think about achieving them if you're sick with anger.

If you think you might have the slightest touch of anger, I'd like to offer you a WebMD-like list of the symptoms of anger and then, in the next chapter, I'll give you a prescription to get rid of it.

DO YOU HAVE ANGER?

Tell me if this sounds like you: From the moment you open your eyes in the morning and you swing your legs out of bed to touch your feet to the ground, you think of some-one or something that's upset you. Your stomach begins to churn, your heart starts racing, and you feel your hands begin to clench.

As you're getting ready in the morning, you can't stop

thinking about it. It begins to make you feel irritated or irrational. Maybe your dog has an accident in the house, and you explode for no reason. Or you get in your car, and it seems like everyone you see that morning is an idiot. "Get in your own lane, loser!" you say as you pass by. But maybe you didn't say the word *loser*, and maybe you even gave them an unkind gesture with a particular finger that's considered offensive.

Or maybe it's something more subtle. Perhaps you stumble upon a photo of a friend or relative on social media whom you had a falling out with. You think thoughts like *Get a life* or *This will teach you* as you graze by without giving a "like." But that person comes back into your mind over and over. And it becomes a snowball racing downhill, getting bigger and bigger.

Life is full of moments that can anger us. That's what makes life life. It's what sparked that famous bumper sticker that says, LIFE HAPPENS. And these "life happens" moments aren't few and far between. If we're not careful, these moments tend to seep into other areas of our life until anger is infecting our relationships.

Anger carries a lot of symptoms, and we all express anger in different ways. Especially when it comes to men and women. Researchers at the American Psychological Association decided to put this theory to the test. They studied over forty thousand men and women to find out how they cope and deal with stress, depression, and negative thoughts—in other words, anger.

The researchers found that women tend to internalize

their anger. Like a bubbling and boiling volcano, women, in most cases, keep everything tucked tightly inside. For example, women will many times stew for years on the same negative thought about something or someone. In fact, when a woman has a disagreement with someone, she'll remember exactly what was said and even what the person was wearing when it happened. These thoughts and feelings will build and build, until one day the volcanic eruption of anger spews out. Often in destructive ways.

Men, on the other hand, tend to be a bit more irrational. The researchers found that men will often externalize their anger. Instead of keeping it bottled up inside, men like to get rid of their anger almost instantaneously. Do you hear of women punching holes in their walls when they're angry? Not often. Angry men like to turn into Mr. Fix-Its. They look at what they might perceive as the root of the problem and try to fight it at all costs. Men with too much anger will oftentimes act out their frustrations in dangerous and inappropriate ways. Maybe through alcohol or physical abuse.

For another great example of how men and women process anger differently, you have to go back to the elementary school playground. When two ten-year-old boys fight, it's intense. Emotions go from zero to sixty in three seconds and top out at speeds of a hundred miles per hour. Punches are thrown, and the fight usually ends up with the gym teacher having to separate the two feuding warriors. But after a stern talking to by the principal and an apology, the most incredible thing happens. Within hours of the dust settling, the boys walk down the hall arm in arm, laughing like best friends. The fight was over the minute it was over. Because everything was left out in the open.

But when two ten-year-old girls fight, there's a lot more involved. Unlike men's, their emotions often go on cruise control at a smooth sixty-five and can stay like that for miles. Girls hold their feelings inside. They hold grudges and talk about one another behind their backs for months at a time. You almost never see two girls arm in arm immediately after a conflict. In many cases, girls can carry negative feelings about one another for years to come.

There's nothing wrong with either approach. In fact, it's the way God designed us to naturally deal with anger. It's what makes up our DNA as men and women. But issues occur when these thoughts and feelings linger. They create a snowball effect. And many times, we don't even know what's to blame. We tend to mistake anger for other emotions. I certainly have. Anger has the unique ability to camouflage itself and act out through other emotional issues. Some of the more popular ones are frustration, disappointment, heartbreak, fear, criticism, unmet expectations, and worry.

MY EXPERIENCE WITH ANGER

I was teased a lot growing up. Mostly by the other guys in my class. Their insults at first just felt like foam Nerf gun bullets, but as I got older and into high school, they felt like arrows laced with poison. I was like a fish out of water when trying to fit in with the other boys in school. While the other guys' worlds mostly revolved around playing basketball and football and chasing girls, I was more interested in photography, charity work, and my family. And to make me stick out even more, my personality is more tenderhearted—so I didn't do well with the whole male insult-bonding thing. My voice was higher than the other guys', I played on the golf team, and all the pretty girls saw me as their best friend and big brother. My home turf was the friend zone.

As you can imagine, this caused some major tension between me and the other guys at school. Not only did they not understand me, but they made it a point to discourage and alienate me because I was different. All these years later, I realize that they were trying to fit me into their box, but I was way out in another stratosphere.

I could take all of the petty insults about things like my high voice and my ridiculous attempts to dribble a basketball. But the ones that really hurt came when people began questioning my sexuality. When I was a freshman in high school, I overheard it for the first time, at the lunch table: "Why do you think Michael Gibson never dates any girls?" one of the guys asked.

"Well, it's obviously because he's gay," said the others.

That one hit me like a ton of bricks. *Gay?* I remember thinking to myself. *Why would they think that?*

It turns out that my voice, athletic ineptitude, and interest in nonsports-related stuff were my prerequisites for being called such. I also had made the decision to hold off on dating through high school, because I had seen how even my friends who were deeply involved in church and their relationships with Jesus made some tough decisions they are still working through today.

Because of this, I was labeled as different. I found myself excluded from parties and social gatherings. I wasn't part of the A-list popular group, and I lived every day with a reputation that seemed to follow me into everything I did.

As the teasing continued, I began to feel different. My joy had vanished. I wasn't treating my parents and sisters with respect. My interest in family traditions, like decorating the Christmas tree and hunting for Easter eggs, disappeared. I suppressed my personality. And I started to resent the people who cared about me and saw me for who I was. Instead I cared only about trying to impress a tiny group of people and desperately prove that I wasn't who they said I was.

I also began to make some mistakes in my character. My language at one point was so bad that a kid on my golf team came up to me after we finished practice one day and asked me if I really was a follower of Jesus, because my words and actions didn't show it. I remember looking at him after he said that, wondering why he would ever say such a thing.

Without knowing it, I found myself in the clutches of anger. My emotions went into shut-down mode. And I needed out.

THE REALITY OF ANGER

Anger is our response to lies we believe about ourselves. While I was stuck in my anger pit, I began to sink deeper and deeper because I began to believe the lies that were being told about me—lies about who I was, who I liked, and what my destiny held. This "reality" I was living in was fake.

I believe that anger is one of Satan's biggest tools to throw us off track. It's one of his most favorite footholds, perfect for sabotaging our relationships. He uses it to deceive us and make us believe in a disturbing alternate reality that just isn't true. In my case, I began to believe that I wasn't worthy of having deep friendships with friends my age and that I was never going to fall in love with a woman and get married someday because everyone assumed I was "gay." I was stuck in a rut that I just couldn't seem to climb out of.

I wasn't alone. It always amazes me how the Lord never fails to send the right person to meet me just where I'm at. Someone who has walked the path before me, who can act as a guide. I met my buddy Brandon while attending a community college in Los Angeles. In a school that was divided by gangs (not an exaggeration here), Brandon and I were from a similar background. He shared with me that he attended an awesome, thriving church in the Los Angeles area and that he was working on getting his associates degree so that he could work on the media team at his church. So when it came to group projects, Brandon and I always partnered up.

We were in a public speaking course together. Which meant we had to give several prepared speeches. In one particular class, our professor mentioned that we had to do a five-minute presentation about our partner. Topics ranged from where they were from and what they wanted to major in to a unique fact about them. We had just one day to come up with our speech; it was due the next class period.

Brandon invited me to grab lunch after class at his favorite taco spot in Sherman Oaks to work on the project. As I began to interview Brandon, I immediately picked up on the fact that he'd had a rough upbringing. He shared with me that his father left him and his mom when he was four years old and that they were all on their own. Money was tight most years, and his mom worked hard to provide for their family. To make matters worse, his mom had married a few other guys, who came and went.

Brandon then began to share his testimony with me. He had tried to seek out the love he was missing from his father in other ways, like with drugs, alcohol, and pornography. He told me that he went from relationship to relationship, each ending in disaster.

Everything changed when a buddy of his invited him to church. That Sunday, he was saved and dedicated his life to Jesus. But after the service and as the weeks went by, Brandon told me, he began to realize that these habits, like pornography and dating around, didn't end. After some soul searching, God revealed to him that there was hate in his heart and an anger that wasn't going to go away without his realizing the root cause.

Brandon stopped in the middle of his story and asked me a sobering question. "Have you ever hated anyone?" he asked.

I shrugged my shoulders and told him that I didn't hate anyone. He pressed harder. He asked me if there was anyone who had rejected me, offended me, or teased me growing up. It hit me. There was anger in my heart toward those boys who had teased me and resented me all through high school. I had never dealt with it properly. I began to share with Brandon all the hardships I had faced in high school and the things this group of guys had said.

Brandon then asked, "Well, was that stuff true?"

"No!" I said loudly. "None of it was true."

"Then why do you continue to carry it?" he asked.

Brandon was right. Ever since high school, I had been carrying the lies these boys told me. And the enemy just picked up where they left off. For four years those lies rang like bells in my brain and heart. When someone rejected me, it was because I wasn't good enough. When someone reached out, I usually resisted because I had built a solid stone wall in my heart to protect me from getting hurt again. Remember those symptoms of anger I mentioned earlier? I'm pretty sure I experienced each one. Frustration because of the rumors and words those guys spread. Disappointment from not being accepted into the "cool" group. Heartbreak because of the constant rejection. Fear and anxiety from jumping into any relationship for the fear of getting rejected. The list goes on and on.

There, sitting over a Mexican lunch with my new buddy Brandon, I realized that it was all a bunch of lies. I was living in a gross alternate reality, created by the lies of the devil, that was different from the purpose God had for my life. I had let it affect who I was. That all changed when I began to look at the truth.

I began to ask, *What is really the truth here?* I'm not gay.
I'm not boring to hang out with. Just because I'm bad at
sports doesn't mean that I'm a useless outcast. I have other
gifts and talents that make me unique. Most importantly,
I am a child of God. He loves me, and He created me to
do great things through Jesus Christ, and to be involved in
deep, true, and real relationships.

The more I began to realize what the truth was, the
more I felt I was again seeing life with clear vision. The
anger that had taken root in my heart was ripped out and
thrown away.

SAYING GOODBYE TO ANGER

We were not created to be angry. Though it is natural to
feel angry from time to time, we weren't designed to harbor it. Think of your car. You would never put water in
your gas tank. Your car needs the right fuel to operate and
work properly. But if you kept putting water in your tank
instead, not only would it not operate, it would end up rust-
ing and be ruined forever.

The same goes for us and anger. We weren't designed to
hold it in for long. Remember what I shared in the introduction about my meeting with Dr. Caroline Leaf, the world-
famous neuroscientist? In her presentation, she showed our
group MRI scans of a brain from someone who did love
well. You could literally see the brain's neurons, the little
treelike stems that send messages to our body, light up like

a Christmas tree. As opposed to someone who chose not to love well: The brain was silent. Zero stimulation detected. And the neurons whittled away. Halfway through her presentation, she stopped and said, "You know, the brain was really only created to do one thing. And when the brain does it really well, you operate at your highest capacity. The brain was created for love."

We were created to process anger, but not carry it. If we allow lie after lie to stay in our heart and spread throughout our thoughts, this deadly emotion begins to decay our spirit, soul, and body. It's no wonder the Apostle Paul is so clear about getting rid of anger in our lives.

> Go ahead and be angry. You do well to be angry—but don't use your anger as fuel for revenge. And don't stay angry. Don't go to bed angry. Don't give the Devil that kind of foothold in your life. (Ephesians 4:26–27)

If you have been walking down some dark paths recently, or if there is some sin in your relationships that you just can't seem to shake, let me ask you the same question Brandon asked me that day over tacos. Do you hate anyone?

We hate the idea of hating people, don't we? Hate is today's deadliest sin. It goes against everything that we're taught and what society says we shouldn't do. But we do it anyway. So let me ask in a different way. Is there anyone who caused a speed bump in your life? Someone who rejected you, hurt you, or made you feel small? Is there someone who abandoned you or disappointed you? Someone who cheated you or tricked you into something that was false? Is there someone who lied to you or deceived you?

If you answered yes to any of those questions, then I have some news for you. Most likely, you have anger living inside of you. And you will never achieve real life love with anger alive and well in your heart and mind.

But people still try, and they try hard. Many times, anger is at the root of the mistakes we make in our relationships. Pornography, addictions, cheating, abuse, lying, destructive conflict. Unfortunately, we find a lot of ways to harm our relationships. The majority of the time, they are symptoms of anger.

Anger is our response to the lies we believe about ourselves. And if we aren't careful, we begin to take the lies to heart and succumb to their treachery. Even scarier, we begin looking for ways to complete this alternate reality and find love where love doesn't exist. That's where anger begins.

If we have anger in our hearts, we begin to look for love in things like pornography, serial dating, and relationships with the wrong people that hinder rather than help us. But those relationships or actions will never satisfy you, because those relationships are built on the lies of anger.

Take it from Brandon. His father abandoning him was tough. Seeing his mother struggle for years to put food on the table was hard to watch. Having different men come into his home and then go right back out again after yet another failed marriage took a toll on his heart and emotions. So he began to believe the lie, the lie that no one wanted him or loved him. After all, his father threw in the towel on him. Why wouldn't others do the same? This led to some poor decisions. One after the other, Brandon was looking for love in all the wrong places. And anger began to breed in his heart.

Anger brings nothing but destruction and pain. But the good news is that though anger is deadly to our bodies and relationships alike, it isn't terminal. If we identify it and realize it's there, we can begin to work on it. There is a powerful antidote and treatment for this disease, a prescription that was given to me by my grandfather. And I promise I'll share it with you. Let's continue our journey of healing in Chapter 3.

Forgiveness

Choosing not to forgive your offenders is like drinking poison and hoping the other person gets sick.

It's hard to believe that there was a time when the common cold was a life-threatening disease. Hundreds of thousands of adults and children alike died each year because of sicknesses that today we couldn't care less about. Today a stuffy nose and sore throat is hardly an excuse for calling in sick. We're expected to pop some Advil and power through.

But as recently as the 1920s, these symptoms were taken much more seriously. Bacterial meningitis, strep throat, and ear infections killed thousands. And the ones who survived were often left with lasting disabilities that they carried until death. Other, more serious infections like tuberculosis, pneumonia, and whooping cough spread like wildfire when an outbreak occurred, taking a serious toll on the population.

Then, in the 1920s, a miracle happened. By accident, British scientist Alexander Fleming discovered a substance that fought bacteria and had the potential to bring simple illnesses to their knees. Using mold, he was able to kill and destroy serious strands of bacteria like *Staphylococcus aureus* (which we call a staph infection). He called his special mold "penicillin." By 1941 penicillin was saving countless lives. Today, because of Fleming's noble achievement, these sicknesses that were once life-threatening can be treated with something as small as a pill. Because of antibiotics, people are alive today who would have died just eighty years earlier.

THE SCIENCE OF FORGIVENESS

In the last chapter, we talked about the disease that's been tearing relationships apart for centuries. We've seen what can happen when we allow anger to seep into our lives and the destruction it brings with it. But here's the hope: There is a cure. And just like antibiotics, it's no less than a miracle.

How are we able to find healing from this infectious disease? If we aren't supposed to let the sun go down on our anger, and instead quickly get rid of it, how do we empty it out of our hearts and minds each day in order to remain healthy? It's by taking a daily dose of *forgiveness*.

Forgiveness isn't something to take for granted. And it's the only true way to rid your heart of the anger that resides within. It's powerful. Proven. And tested by time. Jesus taught that forgiveness is a key to receiving the gift, the gift of salvation and living in relational harmony.

> This is how I want you to conduct yourself in these matters. If you enter your place of worship and, about to make an offering, you suddenly remember a grudge a friend has against you, abandon your offering, leave immediately, go to this friend and make things right. Then and only then, come back and work things out with God. (Matthew 5:23–24)

Before we continue with this first step of forgiveness, let me preface this conversation by saying that if you are the victim of physical or sexual abuse, and if your anger is toward the offender, then I want you to hear this: It's not your fault. You, or something you did, are not the cause of any crime. Those are acts of pure evil. But it is important that you hear this: You cannot continue to harbor anger for that person. I want to challenge you to seek Jesus in prayer and in His Word. Ask the Great Healer to help you experience true freedom by forgiving that person. This is your chance to cut anger off at its knees before it gains a foothold.

You can't afford not to forgive. Yes, it's hard. It puts our pride on the line. And it goes against what we were taught. An eye for an eye! Right? Wrong. Choosing not to forgive your offenders is like drinking poison and hoping the other person gets sick. You are dealing with the effects of anger. You are living the lie—not them. Sure, they have their issues. But it's not your responsibility to nitpick. If you want to experience relational harmony, then stop living in the fairy-tale that everyone gets what they deserve, and you'll end up alright. One way or another, anger has a habit of bubbling up to the top and sabotaging your life and relationships. It doesn't just go away.

Recently, a friend of mine who went through a divorce was sharing with me how she was dealing poorly with being alone. She told me that God hadn't blessed her with the gift of anger yet. And she didn't understand why. The gift of anger? I wanted to explode with words of caution. I felt like screaming, *Thank God! Anger isn't a gift!*

In fact, saying that anger is a gift is the equivalent of saying "I don't know why God hasn't blessed me with cancer." But she brings up a good point. I've heard many people say that anger brings focus and clarity to their work life and helps them move on. People say it makes them stronger. But that's just part of the sick alternate reality and lie the devil likes to use to bring us down. He's not backing down when you enter into that mindset. In fact, he's strengthening the foothold.

Anger lives a lie. And if we're going to experience satisfying and fulfilling relationships, anger has got to go. Then forgiveness needs to enter the picture. But how exactly do we forgive?

LOGS IN YOUR EYE

But you don't know what they did to me.
You don't know what they said.
You don't know how hard it's been for me.

Do those sentences sound familiar? If you're resisting this idea of forgiveness, let me ask, What's stopping you? If you're like millions of other people around the world, you start playing the blame game, which uses a lot of words like "but they" or "but he" and "but she." We seem to become like Supreme Court justices, judging our offender while we stand on a pedestal of our own perfection. Like we are the ones who should decide the fate of our offenders. The first step on our journey of forgiveness is a humbling one. It's also, in many cases, the most difficult and takes the longest to accomplish.

Forgiving others for their wrongdoing toward you starts with examining your own heart. Jesus makes this clear in His gospel: "But if you refuse to forgive others, your Father will not forgive your sins" (Matt. 6:15 NLT).

That sums it up well. Many times, what blocks us from taking the step of truly forgiving is failing to look at our own selves first. We fail to ask the question "What am I at fault for here?" Because often when we are irritated with someone, or refuse to offer grace, these frustrations are reflections of our own immaturity or blind spots caused by "logs" in our eyes. We can choose to use this hurt as an opportunity for growth—or we can continue down a spiraling blame game path until our hearts are taken over by anger.

Remember my friend Brandon from the last chapter? And how poorly he was treated by his dad? Brandon could have easily gone down the wrong path. He could have blamed his dad at every turn: for his future marriage falling apart, all because of not having his dad around as a role model; for not getting a promotion at work, because if his dad hadn't abandoned him, he would have the skill set and confidence to achieve at his job; for dishonoring his children, all because his dad never engaged or tried to be a special part of his life.

Brandon had a lot of excuses because of how his dad treated him. And for a long time, Brandon found it hard to search inside his soul. He hated his father with every fiber of his being. He once vowed that if his dad ever showed his face one day, he would deck him square in the nose. But then he met Jesus and everything changed. His outlook on his dad took a U-turn.

It started with his youth pastor, who asked him if he'd ever taken the time to really examine the way he talked about his father. Brandon couldn't have cared less. It's not like his dad was around to hear it anyway. But Brandon's youth pastor challenged him to search his heart and find some ways that he could honor his dad. Honor? The man who abandoned him? Seemed like a far-fetched plan. But Brandon decided to trust his youth pastor's wisdom, and he began to explore what was causing this roadblock and where the hate was pouring in from.

Sitting down with a pencil and piece of notebook paper, Brandon tried to think of some positives. Nothing came to mind for the first few minutes, but as he began to think harder, thoughts formed. First item on his list? His father was a part of giving him life. Without his father, he wouldn't be alive today. Secondly, his dad brought his family to Southern California, where Brandon would eventually find Jesus in a church. One by one, Brandon began filling his list with positives to honor.

Then it hit him. All these years, he had been passing the blame for his own hardships and trials to his father. Brandon had bashed this man since he walked out the door on his family when Brandon was a little boy. It was Brandon's anger that was preventing him from truly finding forgiveness, not his father's sins.

It may seem sort of backward to look inward for things you can seek forgiveness for. Especially when taking into consideration all the hurt and pain you've experienced. But by eliminating blame and the log in your eye, you can start down the path of healing.

STEPS TO FORGIVENESS

Shortly before Brandon and I met during our public speaking class, he saw his dad for the first time in over sixteen years. Brandon's father had been living in Arizona, working a dead-end job. He had also remarried several times, but each relationship ended like his first: in divorce. After his eye-opening conversation with his youth pastor and discovering the logs of anger and bitterness toward his dad in his own eye, Brandon received a unique message on Facebook.

Brandon's father sent him a private message saying that he was coming to Los Angeles and wanted to meet with him. Brandon's heart skipped a beat. His stomach started to churn. There he was: the man he had resented and hated for years, reaching out, wanting to get together.

Brandon told me that he resisted every urge to simply reply no, block him on social media, and put him out of his life forever. But something was nagging at his heart. Something was shouting in his soul to say "Sure." Which he did.

The three typing dots appeared at the bottom of his screen. His father was writing a reply.

"Great," it said. "Where should we meet?"

"How about a taco?" replied Brandon. "Next Tuesday. I'll send you the address."

All week, Brandon was a nervous wreck. What would his father say? What would he look like? Would he apologize for all those years of being absent? Would he just come up with a bunch of excuses? Brandon didn't know what to feel. He was scared, elated, and confused all at the same time. Why was his dad showing up now? Why was he reaching out?

Brandon went back and forth with himself for an entire week. So much so that he reached out to his youth pastor for guidance. Not knowing what to do or what to say, his youth pastor gave him his best advice: "Just tell him how sorry you are for all the things you've thought and said about him behind his back over the years."

Apologize? No way. This was the man who had betrayed him when he was only four years old. No way was he going to ask for his father's forgiveness. But Brandon's youth pastor talked about how Jesus encourages us to make things right with the person we hold a grudge toward, knowing that this is the only way we will receive the gift. The gift of a love that is true.

It was a humbling opportunity. But Brandon felt ready.

The next day as he entered the taco restaurant, Brandon recognized his dad almost immediately. He was sitting in a booth, staring straight forward. Brandon had never seen his dad like this: scruffy, skin wrinkled and like coarse brown leather from working long hours in the sun, light gray stubble on his face. He wore jeans and an old flannel button-down shirt that had seen better days. In fact, the shirt resembled the man wearing it.

"Hey, Dad," Brandon said.

Standing up, his father offered his son a handshake. Brandon slid into the opposite seat, and there they sat. Neither said a word. His dad just stared at him.

"Dad," Brandon interrupted the silence, "before we start talking about this and that and about what's happened all these years, I just want to say something to you."

Brandon's dad just sat there. Crossing his arms, he braced for the worst.

"Dad, I just want to ask you to forgive me. I've really carried a lot of hatred for you all these years. And I blamed a lot on you. But I realize now, after attending church, accepting Jesus Christ as my savior, and discovering His love through my relationship with Him, that our relationship, though we've been apart, has been strained because of me. I never wanted to reach out, and never wanted a piece of you. I just wanted to ask you to forgive me, for all the foul language I've used against you. All the hurt I blamed on you. Will you ever forgive me?"

Brandon's dad looked across the table at his son, not believing what was coming out of his mouth. His next move shocked Brandon. He pushed the table out of his way, jumped up, and put his arms around his son. Tears streamed down his face. Brandon began to cry too.

"Son, you shouldn't be the one asking for forgiveness," he said. "I came all this way to see you and ask if I could have a do-over. Your mom and you didn't deserve the way I treated you. Would you forgive me?"

And just like that the anger that had festered in both of their hearts for years suddenly evaporated. To make the story even better, Brandon's dad was so moved by the love his son displayed toward him, when he'd been anticipating a blow-out argument, he asked Brandon for that same source of love. Right there, Brandon led his father to the Lord.

Though Brandon and I don't talk as much as we used to, I stumble upon his social media posts. Today, Brandon is twenty-four years old. He's married and has a daughter. And I can happily say that his father, who struggled with years of addiction and anger from his own past relationships, is in his son's life and loves his granddaughter deeply.

I'm thankful for Brandon's story. It proves Jesus' point that if we break down the walls of pride and look through the rubble to see what we might be responsible for, we can partake in the gift that God has given us: true, real relationships with the people in our lives and the people yet to be in our lives.

Brandon also gives us a great picture of what an apology looks like. We all need a bit of help when formulating the right apology. Sometimes it just doesn't roll off the tongue right, so I'd like to offer you five simple steps that I learned from my grandfather for giving a good apology.

1. Be gentle.	Remember, you probably have egg on your face and logs in your eyes. Don't play the blame game. Admit any wrongdoings you can think of first. And be gentle about it.
2. Be open to learning.	Try to increase your understanding of the hurt and pain the other person might be experiencing. Remember, anger lives where truth does not. Understand the context of why the harm might have happened.
3. Admit wrongs.	Here's the truth: It takes two to tango. Chances are there's something you need to admit to. Whether you are the one apologizing or the receiver, it's good to clear the air and admit the wrongs God has laid on your heart.
4. Seek forgiveness with no expectations.	This is a hard one. Brandon's dad could have exploded after discovering his son had been trash-talking him all those years. And on the flip side, Brandon could have said that he wasn't ready to forgive his dad. It's important to allow both parties to process their feelings.

5. Touch each other.	Once you've talked it out, hug it out, high five, hold hands, touch each other's shoulders. Whatever you deem appropriate. Physical touch is a great gauge of how open the other person is to you. Notice how both Brandon and his dad hugged it out and cried tears of joy. Both hearts were wide-open toward each other.

Why wait a single minute to forgive your offender? Or allow them to forgive you? Life is too short to wait. And you don't know what blessing is around the corner, on the other side of forgiveness. It could even lead to an opportunity for greater intimacy and a deeper relationship with the person you forgave. I can't think of a better practice now to ready yourself for marriage and children someday. If you can learn this now, you'll set your relational destiny on the right foot for years to come.

FORGIVING THE UNSEEN

Some of us don't have the luxury of being able to look our offender in the eye and say, "I forgive you" or "Will you forgive me?" Sometimes your offenders might not be safe people to talk to or be around. Or maybe they've passed into eternity. But you can't allow this to be an excuse for passing up forgiveness and allowing anger to take up permanent residence in your heart. Because you're still stuck with it.

Your offenders will be judged someday for their part. But you are still responsible for yours.

Brandon's story of forgiveness really convinced me to look at the logs in my eye and reexamine any anger that might be festering in my heart. I realized that those boys who teased me through high school still touched a nerve. Everything inside of me wanted to prove them wrong and get back at them one day. I used to imagine myself marrying a famous movie star or model and returning to my high school reunion to rub it in their faces.

But if Brandon could forgive his father, who abandoned him and caused him pain for decades, then I could work on forgiving my offenders. But how was I supposed to accomplish this? For all I knew, those guys were spread out throughout the country. Getting them in one spot would be next to impossible.

My grandfather gave me some advice I'd like to share with you. When he was just starting out in ministry, he had a mentor who betrayed him, humiliated him, and almost forced him to abandon the calling God had placed on his life. It was a bad situation. And it left my grandpa with deep wounds of anger.

One day, while sitting in his church office in Waco, Texas, he started thinking about this mentor. Thought after thought entered his head about how awfully this man had treated him and how he would one day seek revenge and bring to light all this man had done to him. But God had different plans. Anger seethed inside my grandpa's heart, and it needed to be released.

The answer came in a surprising way. As an associate pastor at his church, my grandfather often had people in and out of his office. One day a church member came to meet about a potential building project the church was pursuing. The conversation was very straightforward, nothing out of the ordinary. But as the man was leaving the office, he reached into his pocket and pulled out an article he had cut from a magazine. "Would you read this article about forgiveness?" asked the man.

Grandpa was shocked. *Why would this guy give me an article on forgiveness?*

Then the man said that he needed help forgiving someone who had caused him years of pain and had betrayed him multiple times.

"I'm sure you're really good at this," said the man. "Would you read it and meet with me later?"

That was a sobering statement. My grandpa realized that he was harboring real anger toward his mentor. And it was spilling into all areas of his life: his marriage, his parenting, and even his friendships.

When I was struggling with my pain and the anger I carried for my classmates, my grandpa gave me that same article. He had kept it all those years. The advice seemed a little strange, but he said that it gave him immense freedom. This advice was a gift from God.

The article said to imagine there are two people in the room: Jesus and the person you hate. Even rearrange the furniture to have one chair for Jesus and chairs for whomever you need to forgive. I know. It sounds nuts. But wait until you see the healing power of this simple yet effective exercise.

With my grandpa standing next to me during the process, coaching me through, I began saying out loud every offense, every hurt, every painful word those boys ever said about me. One thing after the other, I said each one like it had happened yesterday. At one point, I was practically yelling at a group of empty chairs. Though it had been over two years since I had seen them, the pain was still so fresh.

I vented every detail. *You wrongly accused me and dishonored me in front of my peers. You found different ways to tease me and reject me. You made up lies about me and sold them like they were truth.*

Then my grandpa gently told me to imagine Jesus saying to the guys who offended me, "Do you understand?" And the offenders saying, "Yes."

I pictured Jesus then saying to me, "Michael, do you forgive these boys?"

"Yes," I said softly.

Suddenly, I could feel their words fly out of my mind and heart like doves. Their power was lost. After I forgave their hurts, Grandpa asked me if there was anything that I did to offend these boys. I realized there was.

Through my anger, I had forgotten about the times when I gossiped behind their backs. The times when I judged them for being "scum of the earth." And the times that I manipulated them and lied to them about who I was. Wow. I was almost as bad as them. In fact, the same stuff they did to me, I in turn did right back.

I had some serious logs in my eye, and they needed to come out. I confessed them that day to the Lord Jesus and to my offenders, imagining they were all in the room with me. I discovered that to forgive these guys, I needed to be forgiven. I pictured Jesus asking the guys if they forgave me. And they accepted.

FORGIVE AND KEEP FORGIVING

As we rearranged the furniture back to its original position, my grandpa asked me how I felt. Though it felt good to get that all out, nothing felt any different. I was hoping for an aha moment. But nothing happened. After about an hour or so of playing out this silly exercise, I still didn't feel any different.

"You will in time," my grandpa told me.

Though I was skeptical, I trusted him. Then, several weeks later, quietly and unexpectedly, I was free. My soul felt as light as a feather. No longer did those boys' offenses come to my mind. Joy moved back in where sorrow once resided. Love came back and replaced my anger. I felt free to pursue friendships and relationships in college without anything holding me back.

Grandpa was right. Time doesn't heal all wounds—only forgiveness can. Little by little, my life continued to change. I experienced blessings from God. He gave me opportunities that I only dreamed about in high school. He led me through college and gave me the opportunity to do what I loved: be on television. Once I gave up on the lie that had consumed my heart and started living my true self, my relationships started to flourish again. The friends I made in college are among the greatest of my life. I am free to be me. I'm a living testament that when you are willing to forgive and let go of anger, God opens up a whole new world of wondrous adventures and opportunities.

Though the memories of the teasing I went through in high school still come to mind from time to time, they leave right away. A friend told me recently that he hates the phrase "forgive and forget," because how can we possibly erase painful memories from our minds permanently? They're bound to bubble to the top at some point in life. But what should stop you from continuing to forgive? Each time your offender comes to mind, you have the incredible opportunity to continue forgiving. Through each and every sting, it's our duty to say those sacred words: *I forgive you.*

Have you ever wondered why ducks are able to swim on top of water? With their feathers perfectly dry and not bogged down? Ducks and other types of water birds have unique and special feathers that are coated in a waxy layer that repels water. So when they swoop down from the air into a lake or stream or dive for their next meal underwater, the water never stays on their backs and feathers. It simply rolls off as tiny droplets back into the water, allowing them to stay light and buoyant.

Just like the water droplets that roll off a duck's back, so will the offenses that you forgive roll off yours. Even after forgiving, some people hang on to the offense and carry it all their lives. They hold grudges toward their offender and aren't willing to break down the barriers and honor them. This makes the entire forgiveness process completely backfire.

When you forgive someone, your conflict is done. The offense becomes null and void in your heart. You no longer have permission to spend another second agonizing over what was done to you. Once you say those sacred words, *I forgive you*, your heart enters a new place, a place of healing and of freedom.

DRAINING ANGER

But what if the person we love the most suffers from anger? What can I do?

If you find yourself asking those two questions, I applaud you. And also hurt for you. If you find yourself living life with someone who is angry, it is and will be one of the hardest things you go through. But there's hope for you too.

When I was infected with anger, I didn't know I had companions on my journey of forgiveness—several in fact: my grandpa, my mom, and my sisters. Each played an important role in my healing. But one stuck out. My dad.

While the angry person has to make the decision to heal from their anger, as a companion to an angry person, you have the ability to help drain the anger from that person. In my story, I had to make the decision to forgive those boys. In Brandon's story, he had to make the decision to forgive his father.

Brandon had a youth pastor who spoke truth and helped him see that need. During my journey, I had my dad. He is a special man. Never once has he ever dishonored me. Has he been tough? You bet. Has he made a mistake here and there? Sure has. But Dad had the wisdom to see that his son was angry. And he decided to be right there with me.

A good parent doesn't turn their back when their child is going through something hard. They get closer. That's exactly what my dad did. We played a lot of golf together through that time. We traveled together when Dad had business. And through those times, we laughed together. Cried together. Got stronger *together*.

Here's the key: It wasn't some miraculous, earth-shattering speech that melted away my anger. It wasn't a special prayer (even though he spent a lot of time on his knees praying for me in private). What helped to drain my anger was the *together* part. Angry people are lonely people. It's a symptom of the disease.

People who are sharing life with and trying to love someone who's angry tend to feel self-conscious, wondering if they're really the right person. Many times during this struggle people back away when they should be getting closer. The truth is you already are the right person for the job. Not as a spiritual giant. Not as the person who always has the right thing to say. Just simply by being you.

God has a way of using our most insignificant qualities for something significant. Our job is just to show up.

The first step to loving someone through anger, whether they're a significant other, family member, or friend, is just to be there. Make them laugh. Take them to dinner. Enjoy their company. And watch as their anger begins to shrivel up little by little.

RICH IN LOVE

Could you imagine if Jesus were to remember all of our sins, offenses, and transgressions against Him? Mine would be a laundry list the size of Texas. But because of the Cross, we are forgiven. Our offenses roll off Jesus' back like water off a duck's. He's not bogged down and barely swimming. He's thriving. He loves us right where we're at. And He doesn't hold it over us. I love how the Psalmist puts it:

> *God is sheer mercy and grace;*
> *not easily angered, he's rich in love.*
> *He doesn't endlessly nag and scold,*
> *nor hold grudges forever.*
> *He doesn't treat us as our sins deserve,*
> *nor pay us back in full for our wrongs.*
> *As high as heaven is over the earth,*
> *so strong is his love to those who fear him.*
> *And as far as sunrise is from sunset,*
> *he has separated us from our sins. (Psalm 103:7–11)*

Wow! What a beautiful testament and textbook definition of forgiveness, right? Jesus is the perfect example of how we are to think about and treat our offenders after forgiveness is complete. And when you forgive, freedom, peace, kindness, and love will flood your heart.

That's where real life love exists.

PART 2

Growing in Love
for God

CHAPTER 4

Celebrating Trials

*What treasures await in the deep
places of your pain?*

Daniel and Jess stood in the muck holding hands and watching as their life floated away. The smell of fresh mud filled their noses. Their rain boots kicked up dirt and twigs as they sloshed around through their once-peaceful neighborhood.

"That's where our mailbox used to be," said Daniel, pointing to a lone wooden post.

Tears welled up in Jess's eyes. This was their first house together. This was the house she and Daniel had picked out and built together. The house that they had worked so hard to save up for, and was now submerged in more than three feet of water. The hours of work to refurbish it, the trips to Magnolia Market in Waco, Texas, to pick out the special decorations Jess had dreamed of, the hours putting them up—all of it now seemed like a waste of time. This was the house where they spent their first blissful year as newlyweds. This house was supposed to be the place they someday brought their future newborn baby home to. The house that their child would take their first steps in. The house that would host birthday parties, Christmas dinners, and hidden Easter eggs. But now it was a stinky mudhole.

Daniel just stood there, expressionless. He'd spent hours searching for this house on Zillow. He'd crunched the numbers and negotiated the perfect price for their budget. He worked with their realtor to get the right monthly mortgage rate. Then he and his buddies spent all night carrying furniture from a U-Haul into his and Jess's new home. This was the American dream. A white picket fence, a charming neighborhood close to good schools. A big backyard for the kids to play in someday. And three bedrooms, two bathrooms. Plenty of space to grow. A dream that was now covered in mold and washed away.

Daniel and Jess had been married just over a year when disaster struck. Graduating from a small college just outside of Dallas, Texas, Daniel was offered a great position as a youth pastor at a church in Beaumont, Texas. But then disaster struck on August 29, 2017, when Hurricane Harvey smashed into the Gulf Coast, leaving a trail of destruction with over $125 billion in damage. And taking the lives of eighty-eight people.

Being born and raised in the Midwest, Daniel and Jess didn't know what to expect as the storm approached. Hurricanes weren't a problem where they were from. Should they ride it out? Or evacuate like their other neighbors? Luckily, at the last minute, Daniel felt that they should evacuate. That decision saved their lives. The new couple watched television storm coverage in shock at Jess's parents' home in Kansas City, Missouri, as their town faced intense flooding. Water rose above cars, street signs, and even homes. They knew their house was probably among them. With it being in an older neighborhood, it was almost certain.

TRIALS . . . A SLIMY OYSTER

What's unfolding in Daniel and Jess's life is a common phenomenon. No, not everyone has to cope with the tragedy of losing everything they have in floods and hurricanes. But everyone goes through hard times at some point in their life. In fact, we can go through hard times daily. They're called *trials*.

Trials frequent our daily life. Whether we like it or not, something is bound to go wrong in our day. Something is bound to cause stress, be difficult, or find some way to annoy us. And they vary in scale. Trials can be as light as the car in front of you not turning when the traffic light turns green, or as heavy as losing a loved one in a terrible accident. You just don't know what's coming your way. But one thing is for sure: Trials happen.

The term *trial* is rarely used in today's times. Most of us just refer to these moments as "riding the struggle bus," "going through hard times," or "crap happens" (except some people don't say the word *crap*). But it's important to understand what these moments actually are. *Merriam-Webster's Dictionary* says that trials are "a test of faith, patience, or stamina through subjection to suffering or temptation." A very fair description, I think.

A test of faith? Patience? Or stamina? No thank you. If I had three magic wishes from a genie, I would definitely use all three to get rid of trials in my life permanently. And I'm sure you would too. Who wants to go through pain and suffering all their life? Wouldn't life be so much happier if we just didn't have to deal with the bad, and lived only in the land of good?

It's a nice fairytale, isn't it? But it couldn't be further from reality. The real truth is trials are always with us. They're a constant companion during our life on earth. So if we have to deal with them almost daily, shouldn't we learn how to get along with trials? Shouldn't we try to look at the trials we face with fresh eyes instead of continuing to walk in them blindly?

When I was in the seventh grade, I began the difficult work of looking at the trials in my life differently. Remember that I shared with you about being teased in junior high and high school? Though God healed me of that pain through the power of forgiveness, there was also another element crucial to my journey toward relational peace. It was looking at trials for what they are: slimy, beautiful, messy blessings. Just like an oyster.

SEARCHING FOR HIDDEN TREASURE

Oysters are strange creatures. They live on the ocean floor. And although they are living and breathing things, many mistake them for ordinary rocks. Or something people eat in fancy restaurants. But these incredible creatures also give us one of the most rare and desirable of possessions. A pearl.

The magic begins when one tiny particle of irritating sand somehow manages to lodge itself in the oyster's squishy mouth. Little by little, the oyster covers the piece of sand in its mouth with a special substance that eventually forms a tiny white ball. Which then becomes a pearl.

So what do oysters and pearls have to do with the hard times, or trials, in our life? Think of the hardest thing you've ever had to go through. Allow yourself to feel your emotions from that time. Maybe it was something or someone you lost. Maybe it was a failed business. Or a failed relationship. Maybe someone hurt you. Maybe you felt rejected.

Imagine how that made you feel. You probably felt a whole host of emotions. Maybe you felt angry, upset, and bitter. Now start to picture how that particular situation helped shape the person you are today. Did it make you stronger? Did it make you wiser? Did you avoid a later disaster because of it? Think of how this situation might have made a positive impact in your life today. Think about where you would be today if you hadn't gone through that situation. Are you smarter because of it? Do you have thicker skin? Did you learn something about yourself in the midst of the struggle?

This process of thinking through *how* trials have shaped you will revolutionize your relationships, and it's called treasure hunting.

Searching for treasure in the midst of trials isn't something new. In fact, it's noted all over Scripture. James, Jesus' little brother, mentions the power of taking this new look at trials.

> Consider it a sheer gift, friends, when tests and challenges come at you from all sides. You know that under pressure, your faith-life is forced into the open and shows its true colors. So don't try to get out of anything prematurely. Let it do its work so you become mature and well-developed, not deficient in any way. (James 1:2–4)

James knew that by looking at our difficulties with fresh eyes and faith, these hindrances and difficulties could actually be used for our benefit, and our blessing. They will completely revolutionize the way you look at the world. And how you love others.

Treasure hunting starts much like searching for pearls in oysters. Divers risk their lives searching for these unique creatures in the dark and murky depths of the world's oceans. The same should be done in the deep and dark places of your trials.

When Daniel and Jess took in what had happened, and the devastation that Hurricane Harvey did to their home, they cried out to God to give them an answer for this mess. Why them? Why now? Though they both had great jobs and insurance, some items couldn't be recovered and were expensive to replace. Money wasn't necessarily in abundance for them. What were they to do next? Fear began to take root in their hearts.

As they began to process this while standing there in their rain boots, God did a miraculous thing. All of the negatives that were coming to their minds began to turn to positives. Suddenly, instead of having thoughts like *Why us?* and *We're not going to get through this,* their minds began to play a new tune.

Daniel and Jess began to think about how lucky they were to have survived. If they had made the mistake of "riding out the storm," there's a strong chance they wouldn't be alive today. Then they began to be grateful that they had each other. Both felt more bonded and tightly knit after watching this disaster unfold on television, and now in person. And most importantly, they remembered a verse that Daniel had been teaching the youth at his church.

Do not be anxious about anything, but in everything by prayer and supplication with thanksgiving let your requests be made known to God. And the peace of God, which surpasses all understanding, will guard your hearts and your minds in Christ Jesus. (Philippians 4:6–7 ESV)

Both Daniel and Jess immediately felt a peace that neither had felt before. They had waded through the waters, in the depths of a dark and desolate trial, and found an oyster. And inside the oyster was a beautiful pearl: a pearl of bonding and closeness and of deeper relationships with each other and with Christ.

What treasures await in the deep places of your pain? Finding the oyster is the first step, but you can't just stop there. I don't know about you, but I haven't seen too many oysters in jewelry stores. That's because the pearl diver opened up the crusty, ugly shell and searched inside the slimy goo to find that priceless pearl. Talk about the very definition of finding the positive in a negative!

Just like Daniel and Jess, you can't stop at just finding the oyster. You have to do the important work of opening it up, exposing and exploring the very guts of the situation. Only then does God deliver a pearl. And while you aren't guaranteed to find a pearl inside every real oyster, you are sure to find a pearl in the midst of every trial. You just have to suit up and get in the water.

Jesus promises that if we just get in the water and look for the oyster, we'll find a pearl. Every time. And so much more. The Apostle Paul solidifies this promise in his letter to the Romans: "And we know that for those who love God all things work together for good, for those who are called according to his purpose" (Rom. 8:28 ESV).

Let's face it: Cancer, disease, divorce, and abuse are hard tragedies to swallow, much less experience firsthand. It's difficult to imagine that any of those tragedies could be used for any good. Yet God is bigger than all of those things. He loves us in a way greater than our human minds can understand, and He uses these dark and murky trials to redeem us. He has a life-giving way of restoring anything for our good and for His glory.

Author and speaker Nick Vujicic is a living testament to this promise. Born without arms and legs, Nick came as quite a surprise to his mom and dad. In fact, his mom was a midwife and delivered hundreds of babies. She'd done the ultrasounds, taken the necessary medications and vitamins. But when Nick was born, she and his dad were shocked. It wasn't genetic. And the doctors couldn't find evidence of any disease. He was a medical mystery. But more so than his medical ailments, it was the mystery of how they were supposed to raise their son that Nick's parents faced.

It took several months for them to adjust to their new son. Then soon his parents began to realize how much of a blessing he is. As Nick began to grow up, he learned how to function like any other kid his age. He learned how to brush his teeth and wash his hair. But he was still faced with the harsh reality that he was different from everyone else. His peers didn't let him forget it. Many times, Nick was excluded from games and heard mean comments about him. When he turned ten, Nick had had enough. Contemplating suicide, he no longer wanted to be a burden to his parents. He felt that he was worthless, would never experience the joy of getting married or starting a family. That is, until he met another boy who was just like him, also born with no arms and legs. And Nick began to reach out to this boy to help him.

Nick began to make his life about helping. As a teenager, he began traveling around Australia speaking to kids about how to discover direction in their lives, to understand their values and purpose. He taught kids to face life without fear and understand that they were gifts from God.

Through his teaching, Nick built an international ministry. Today he's spoken in fifty-eight countries and has logged 3 million miles of traveling. And he is married and has a son. Nick was able to turn his depression and trial into joy by discovering the gifts life had to offer. In a recent blog post he wrote for the *Today Show*, Nick said, "We sometimes wait for a miracle to happen in life—but the miracle never comes. I wish many things were different in my life. But knowing I can be a miracle for someone else makes my life worth living. We all have worries. I am not a superhero. But I embrace life and focus on what is most important."

Nick's life hasn't been easy. But he was able to rise above his circumstances and out of the ashes of an extremely challenging trial. Through his motivational speaking and ministry, Nick found his pearl. And it has changed countless lives for the better.

LOVE GROWS FROM TREASURE HUNTING

Trials are the express lane to deeper relationships. If you don't go through tough times in life, then you'll never achieve real life love. Just like a diamond, which starts out looking like a big, ugly rock, your life has to go through pressure. It must be sculpted and shaved down to reveal its sparkly and valuable core.

Without trials, we wouldn't learn anything. Our hearts would remain hardened. We wouldn't be able to see a future for ourselves, because we'd have nothing to base it on. And we wouldn't have the compassion to love people fully and truly. The Apostle Paul recognizes this important place for trials in our life.

> …We rejoice in our sufferings, knowing that suffering produces endurance, and endurance produces character, and character produces hope, and hope does not put us to shame, because God's love has been poured into our hearts through the Holy Spirit who has been given to us. (Romans 5:3–5 ESV)

By experiencing trials and lifting them up to the heavens in high esteem and praise, Jesus literally pours back into our hearts more of His love. By experiencing pain in our lives, we build up stock in love. And whenever we discover a pearl, and the positivity in our pain, then Jesus cashes out on our stock by giving us an endless supply of deeper love and compassion. He even includes an extra bonus of hope and character! In other words, real life love grows in the fertilizer of our pain.

But before we can receive the priceless gifts that Jesus gives us through our pearls, we have to first figure out what we're rejoicing over. That's when the actual treasure hunting comes into play.

In every difficulty, we know that there is a positive, or pearl, that is worthy of celebration, a pearl that is valuable to our character and relational growth. But we first have to find it. Oysters are notoriously tight-lipped. They don't open for just anyone or anything. Many times, treasure hunters have to pry them open to get a peek inside. The same goes for your trial. You have to work hard to pry it open. But the reward is worth the temporary struggle. A great way to start this process is by listing your trial at the top of a piece of paper and then writing the positives down, one by one.

Recently, I went through a tough conflict with a relative that involved a disagreement on a work-related issue. Yes, it was painful and hurtful. And no, I didn't think anything good could come out of it. But I remembered that God promises there is a pearl in every ugly oyster. I knew a positive in the midst of my trial was waiting inside. I just needed to do some prying to release it. Here are some points from my list of the benefits (pearls) from my trial:

- **Wisdom:** I'm smarter and more responsible in the ways that I communicate and coordinate the way I do business. Especially with the ones I love.
- **Compassion:** We all want to be treated with kindness. I learned that compassion speaks louder than words.
- **Empathy:** I understand that we all have issues we're working through. I value the feelings of others and feel compassion for what's hiding under the surface.
- **Grace:** Just like how I want the chance to someday receive grace from people when I am wrong, I get the

opportunity to practice giving grace, which is the greatest gift.

- **Increased Faith:** I get the opportunity to draw closer to Jesus, who then draws nearer to me with support and love. He upholds me in the midst of all storms.

The above pearls are just a few that I found in my oyster. Sometimes trials contain just one beautiful pearl, other times an entire necklace. You never know what treasures are hiding in the depths of your pain. But I promise if you dig deeper and search through the slime, you're going to find one.

CHEERING LOUD FOR ALL TO HEAR

Daniel and Jess and Nick Vujicic had every reason to live life in a dark place. A life full of anger, depression, disbelief, and pain. Losing your home in a once-in-a-lifetime storm? Being born without limbs? I can't imagine facing those trials. Most people in this world would take a long time to get over them, much less begin to see any positive. But each made the choice to treasure hunt. They made the choice to look for the positive and discover the beautiful masterpiece God was writing into their stories.

For Nick, attitude is everything. He had every reason to give up and live life angry, depressed, misunderstood, and believing he just wasn't good enough. But Nick decided to overcome that hurdle and began to see his life through a positive lens. Watching one of his motivational speeches online, I heard Nick say, "We may have absolutely no control over what happens to us, but we can control how we respond. If we choose the right attitude, we can rise above whatever challenges we face."

Your trial doesn't define you, only your attitude toward the trial. And guess what? You are in control of your attitude. No one else and nothing else can control the way you look at your trials. Instead of viewing trials as horrible and difficult situations, think of them as God performing His wonders through you: "Remember the wonders he has done, his miracles, and the judgments he pronounced" (Ps. 105:5 NIV).

When I read that verse, I can't help but think of Nick. Today not only does Nick see the incredible wonders the Lord has done through him, but he celebrates the good. This is the next step in our journey of treasure hunting: finding the courage not only to open the oyster shell and identify the pearl, but to *celebrate*. This is by far the hardest step for me.

In the pain and struggles I've faced, the last thing I feel like doing is cheering. But if we're really going to receive more of God's love, hope, and character, we have to make the decision to do it. This isn't a task for the faint of heart. This is where real life love takes a warrior, a dreamer. It's a brave act. But luckily, we have our Heavenly Father on our side to aid us in this next step.

Before we begin to celebrate, I want to first show you

what you are actually celebrating. The celebration is not in the pain. Pain is just a symptom of the surgery God is doing on your soul. What you are truly celebrating is the benefits. You're celebrating the pearl-making process.

When I first discovered from my grandfather this art of celebrating things I'd once thought weren't worthy of celebration, I didn't quite understand it. This is mostly because our natural human insight can't do it. It's against our nature. Our intuition screams to run away and hide. We're afraid that if we celebrate, the pain and suffering will intensify. What a lie! That's a foothold the enemy uses against us. It's important to understand that pain and suffering aren't punishments God uses to take something from us. He allows us to go through trials so that we might receive more and be more: more strength, hope, and endurance. And we become wise, strong, compassionate people.

I was fourteen when my youngest sister, Zoie, came into my life. She was born in Ethiopia and became my sister when she was six months old. So I was old enough to be her teen dad. Talk about the ultimate birth control! But I clearly remember when my little Ethiopian princess started to learn to walk. I would lie on the floor in our living room for hours, holding her up while she learned to stand. Then, one day, she took a wobbly step. Then another step. Then another. And during the entire process, I kept my hands close by her sides in case she was to fall.

That's how I picture Christ guiding us through our pain. He puts us on the floor. He watches us closely as we stand up. He keeps his hands close by our sides. He wants so desperately to see us take one step, then another, then another until we're walking right into our brightest future. That's why He calls it a *test*. Today, Zoie is on the brink of her teen years. She walks without problems, runs around the yard with our labradoodle, jumps on the trampoline, and rides her bike. But did she start like that? No. She practiced, gained strength, and eventually started walking, like she was designed to do. And she's going to keep getting stronger. Year after year, her legs continue to grow more muscle. They grow longer each day. And one day, she'll be completely grown. Maybe even running the marathon in the Olympics!

That's why we celebrate. That's why we learn to cheer in the midst of trials. Because one baby step at a time, we discover the blessings and we celebrate them even when it feels hard. Blessings like discovering who we truly are in the midst of struggle. Gaining more insight into greatly needed relationship tools like empathy and compassion. And becoming spiritually more reliant and faith-driven toward Christ. Each of these spills into the way we love.

Before we know it, we start loving our families more, our friends more. We start loving the random people we come across. If we're married, we start loving our spouse more. If we have kids, we start loving them more. Not to mention that our character begins to improve. And we have immense hope that when the next storm comes our way, instead of a torrential downpour, we'll see it as a fine drizzle. Because we've gained the hope and supernatural wisdom to know that Jesus is getting us to the other side— every time.

BITTER OR BETTER

When I was first learning this concept from my grandpa, he used to keep a set of cheerleading pom-poms at his house and another in his car. He made sure he had a pair wherever he went. When I would complain about something hard that was happening in my life, or when he caught me being irritated by something, Grandpa would pull out his pom-poms and shake them in the air yelling, "Yay! I can't wait to see how this irritation is going to bless you!" Or "Wow! Go, Michael! You're going to be so blessed for this horrible thing that's happening in your life right now!" It didn't matter where we were, in his car, in the middle of Target, or watching a movie at the theater, he would pull out those pom-poms and celebrate.

Was it annoying? You bet. Embarrassing? No doubt. But after a while, it began to drill into my head. All of a sudden, I started to realize that I was faced with a choice. I could continue to feel sorry for myself, continue to feel like a loser, continue to wallow in self-pity. Or I could grab the bull by the horns, pick myself up, and just keep moving forward. I could choose to stay bitter or become better.

The mantra of "Bitter or Better" is as common a phrase

in my family as "Go, Patriots" or "Go, Cubs" is in other families. Instead of sports cheers, we give "self-help cheers." And it simply means this: *You can stay miserable or choose to be happy.*

The catalyst for this funny phrase came when my grandparents were serving at their first church in Minneapolis, Minnesota, in 1967. My grandpa met a godly pediatrician named Dr. Gerald Brandt, who had found his wife dead from a stroke, lying on their kitchen floor, on his very last day of work. What was supposed to be a day of celebrating his retirement turned into immense sorrow. Anger flooded his heart. His medical career, which lasted almost half a century, had completely consumed their lives. Which is understandable, as a good doctor serves his patients faithfully through thick and thin.

After all those years of work, Dr. Brandt was looking forward to living out his sunset years with his beloved by his side. But on that very afternoon, his dreams were dashed. It took much soul searching, and lots of arguing with God, but then he had a revelation. One day, Dr. Brandt was in yet another screaming match with God when he felt God saying, "Gerald, you can continue to be bitter about this, or you can choose to be better."

A straight shooter with a type-A personality, Dr. Brandt began to take a look at this painful situation in a new light. He began to look to the Almighty for his answers, and made the decision to look for a blessing. Dr. Brandt began to remember all the wonderful memories he had with his wife. The three kids they raised together. And the eight grandkids he now had the new chance to pour his time, energy, and love into. Suddenly, sorrow turned to substance. And he decided to walk out of that trial as a better person, not a bitter one.

Though it has been over fifty years since Dr. Brandt shared that truth with my grandpa, his legacy still lives on in my life. And now in yours. His words make me think of all of the things Jesus had to say about this subject during his ministry on Earth. In fact, in the original Greek translation, Jesus uses the word *rejoice*, one definition of which can be translated to "cheer." Take a look: "These things I have spoken to you, that in Me you may have peace. In the world you will have tribulation; but be of good *cheer*, I have overcome the world" (John 16:33 NKJV, emphasis added).

Jesus encourages us to make the decision to be better. Jesus also tells us that we should expect trials, but in the same breath He also says that we should be intentional about giving a good, loud cheer.

You're blessed when your commitment to God provokes persecution. The persecution drives you even deeper into God's kingdom. Not only that—count yourselves blessed every time people put you down or throw you out or speak lies about you to discredit me. What it means is that the truth is too close for comfort and they are uncomfortable. You can be glad when that happens—give a *cheer*, even!—for though they don't like it, *I* do! And all heaven applauds. And know that you are in good company. My prophets and witnesses have always gotten into this kind of trouble. (Matthew 5:10–12, emphasis added)

Heaven roars when you choose to get up and walk through trials. Jesus is cheering you on. And He's waiting to give you His blessings. He wants to give you more of His love as you not just walk but cheer through the tough times. Why wouldn't you want to be a part of that blessing?

LET THE STORM CALM

Have you noticed a common denominator in each of the stories I've shared in this chapter? After each trial, how did each of these people respond? At first, they grieved. They took the time to feel. They felt all the feelings necessary. It's okay to feel sad. It's okay to feel angry. It's even okay to feel scared. It's natural for us to feel this way. You would have to be a heartless and soulless robot if you didn't feel the pain from your trials. Sometimes the oyster seems too tightly shut for us to open it. It can feel like that jar of marinara sauce that just won't open, no matter how hard you try. It even hurts your hands in the process.

But here's the other common denominator. Each person made the important decision to open it. Oysters can't stay shut forever. One way or another, they will open. And you will see all that's inside. But it's okay if it takes some time. There are trials that I experienced ten, even fifteen years ago that I'm just now discovering pearls from. The key is you have to be willing to open them. You need a willing heart and spirit that says, "God, this is really tough. It doesn't feel like I'm going to get to the other side of this one. But I will keep moving forward, because I know, no matter what, there's going to be a beautiful blessing on the other side." That is how our hearts change and become stronger. We become more loving because of trials. Love pours more love into all of our relationships.

CHAPTER 5

Memorizing God's Word

*The secret to real life love is intertwined
with a real life Savior.*

My first encounter with the power of Scripture and God's Word occurred when I was ten years old. It really saved my tail. I learned about how God's holy and powerful Word can truly transform our relationships.

I wasn't the most studious of students in history. Academics are hard for me. My personality isn't the kind that studies and stays grounded in the tasks at hand. I'm a natural dreamer. I believe that dreaming big dreams is a missed spiritual gift. And I've been dreaming since the third grade.

In the middle of one of my daydreams, probably about the adventures I would have after the school bell rang, I completely forgot about an important class project that was due the next day. I was more interested in the *Lord of the Rings* characters I would act out in my backyard that evening than the lava-flowing volcano I was supposed to create for science class.

The school bell rang, and I quickly ran out of class and directly into my mom's car.

"Did you get all of your homework?" Mom asked.

"Yeah, Mom!" I said. "Let's get out of here!"

Mom put the car in drive and began driving away. The school I attended was really difficult to get in and out of. There was one entrance and one exit, with tons of traffic in between. Just before I made it to complete freedom, my stomach got sick. I had forgotten my science project in my desk. It wasn't the first time.

My forgetfulness was a point of conflict for my mom and me. She couldn't understand how I could be so forgetful. Now that I'm older, it makes total sense. I would have been just as frustrated with me! But I didn't see it that way when I was ten.

"Mom…there's something I need to tell you," I said sheepishly.

"What did you do?" Mom asked.

"I forgot my homework in my desk. Can we please turn back?" I asked.

Mom rolled her eyes. This was the straw that broke the camel's back. Not only did she say we definitely weren't going back—for the gazillionth time—but this time I was grounded. Before I knew it, I found myself in a full-blown lecture series from my mom. I started hearing all about how irresponsible I was and how much I was like my grandfather—head in the clouds and hardly able to focus!

For the record, my mom is the sweetest woman on this earth. But Lord help you if you cross her. She is a strong woman of God, and she has no problem challenging your flaws. Her sermons in these moments are about as passionate as a revival preacher's! And as with a revival preacher's sermon, you'd better plan to be there for a while.

What my mom didn't know was that during the past few months, I had been memorizing Scripture with my grandpa. One day, after yet another lecture from my mom, I had run over to his home and asked him for advice. I thought, *If Grandpa helps millions of other people with their problems, I'm sure he can help me stop my mom from driving me crazy.*

Right then and there, Grandpa decided that I needed some Scripture in my life. He told me that if I memorized five verses, he would take me on a special fishing trip. Right there, I struck a deal that is still blessing me even today.

One of the verses we started memorizing together was from the book of James: "Post this at all the intersections, dear friends: Lead with your ears, follow up with your tongue, and let anger straggle along in the rear" (James 1:19).

Another translation puts it as "be quick to listen."

Ordinarily, I would have responded to my mom's lecture that day by completely engaging in an all-out verbal war with her. Things would have been said. And the length of my grounding would continue to increase. But not this time. Before I knew it, James 1:19 popped into my head: "Lead with your ears, follow with your tongue." Instead of belittling her or defending myself, I just sat there— listening to her words and understanding each one. *Whoa!* I thought. *That's never happened before.*

Then another miracle occurred. As I was listening to my mom, the second verse I had memorized and meditated on with my grandpa popped into my head.

Summing it all up, friends, I'd say you'll do best by filling your minds and meditating on things true, noble, reputable, authentic, compelling, gracious—the best, not the worst; the beautiful, not the ugly; things to praise, not things to curse. (Philippians 4:8–9)

While my mom was talking, and as I was listening to what she was really saying, I instantly felt compassion. I felt empathy for her mommy heart, which I tortured all of the times I forgot to do my assignments and jeopardized my chances of moving on to the next grade. Suddenly, I realized that my mom must care a whole bunch if she's that passionate about my remembering to do my schoolwork. I remembered who my mom was: a valuable, kind, compassionate, giving, tender-hearted person. How could I ever think of criticizing her?

So I thought I'd share what I was feeling. But now I had another problem. I had to interrupt her at the "come-to-Jesus" moment of her sermon.

"Hey, Mom!" I said.

Mom just kept rolling on. Like a steam engine chugging through the plains, she wasn't stopping for anything, or anyone.

"Mom!" I said a little louder.

Still no result. She was almost to the altar call. Finally, I got really loud.

"Mom!" I shouted.

That got her attention.

"Mom, I just wanted to quickly say how thankful I am for what you're saying to me right now. Because it proves to me one more time how much you love me, and how well you want me to do in school. So you can keep going if you'd like."

I braced myself for the worst. But something even more amazing happened. My mom pulled off to the side of the road and started to cry. And laugh. She told me how much she appreciated those words, and that my schooling really does mean the world to her. In fact, she was so moved by what I said, and the love that I demonstrated, that she swung the car around, and we went back to school together to get my science project. We even went out for ice cream afterward.

In the past, our conflicts ended very differently. But this time real life love was demonstrated, and the key was the transforming power of God's Word.

A MISUNDERSTOOD LOVE TOOL

Reading and memorizing the Word of God isn't a new concept. God Himself commanded the ancient Israelites to soak up His great Word and teachings like a sponge.

Love God, your God, with your whole heart: love him
with all that's in you, love him with all you've got!
Write these commandments that I've given you today
on your hearts. Get them inside of you and then get
them inside your children. Talk about them wherever
you are, sitting at home or walking in the street; talk
about them from the time you get up in the morning
to when you fall into bed at night. Tie them on your
hands and foreheads as a reminder; inscribe them on
the doorposts of your homes and on your city gates.
(Deuteronomy 6:5–7)

Memorizing and meditating on God's Word is an act of
love toward Him. And He always reciprocates that love!

By following through on the commandment to write
these important Words on our hearts, surrounding and
covering ourselves with them, we begin to be transformed
from the inside out. Memorizing Scripture at a young age
laid the groundwork for the way I love and was the beginning of the many blessings the Lord placed in my life.

Many of us have grown up hearing about this in youth
groups and Bible studies. In fact, we hear it so often that our
hearts become numb to the advice. I certainly was numb to
it for many years. It wasn't until my senior year of college,
through difficult and trying times, that I decided to invest
and dive deeply into God's sacred text. What could I lose?

In the past, I never understood the importance of spend-
ing time with Jesus. Or really how to do it. Plus, I'm a night
owl. So getting up early in the morning really isn't my

thing. For years, that was my excuse for not reading God's Word. Until a pastor friend encouraged me to try reading one passage of Scripture a day. It could be as long as I wanted, or as short. As long as I cracked my Bible open.

Before I knew it, I was captivated by the Word. Sure, it helped me align my heart and mind for the day. And it gave me an opportunity to hear from God. But it also began to transform my relationships. Oftentimes when I was on the brink of a verbal war with someone, the Scripture I read that day would immediately soften my heart.

Reading God's Word is a sign of spiritual maturity. Because it means you're serious about a life change. Serious about your relationship with God. And the more you do it, the more mature you'll become. If you want to fill your days with real life love, you must take Christ at His word and learn to love reading His Word. After all, who better to learn to love from than the King of Love Himself?

NOT JUST ANOTHER FIVE-STEP PROGRAM

Though I didn't become an active Word reader until I was in my early twenties, I can't help but look back and see how the art of memorizing and meditating on Scripture helped sculpt my life. I believe that because of the verses that I hid in my heart as a young boy, I never tried anything I shouldn't have with girls or hurt the people I love with stupid decisions.

We live in a world that's full of "quick-fix" programs.

Every time I visit a bookstore, I'm overwhelmed by its vast collection of self-help books. Books for fixing your house, making more money, cooking better meals, losing weight, or loving better. These books are created with the best intentions. Heck, this book could even be considered one of them. But if you really want to transform your relationships, you have to start reading God's Word, and you must begin to memorize and meditate on His words.

You could memorize and meditate on the words in this book. But I can adamantly guarantee you that while there might be some good advice in these pages, it'll never transform the way you think or act. The Word of God is alive. This book isn't. The Word of God has transformative power. This book doesn't. And the Word of God speaks to you. While this book can't talk.

Gateway Church in Southlake, Texas, is my home church away from home. My parents live just a few blocks from one of its campuses, so I frequently visit on Sundays when I'm in town. During one sermon, the senior pastor of Gateway, Robert Morris, said something about the Word of God that shook me to my core. He said that if you fail to understand that the Word of God is a spiritual book, written by a spiritual being to spiritual beings, then you will never understand the Bible. The natural mind can't understand it, because this powerful book speaks to our souls, our thoughts, and our hearts.

Pastor Robert in this same sermon compared the Bible to food and water. Experts estimate that our bodies can go between forty and sixty days without food. That's a lot of days. But we wouldn't make it three days without water. Just like how food and water nourish our bodies, so does the Bible our soul. It has the power to go beyond us and transform our lives through Christ Jesus.

So if you're looking for a quick-fix method to solve your relationship issues, I have some bad news for you. This book can't fix them alone. While I believe wholeheartedly in the power of the seven principles I've organized this book around, and that they are inspired by God, I alone can't help you. Only Jesus can. And only through the power of His great Word.

TRANSFORMATION IS POSSIBLE

If you're intimidated by the awesome power of the Bible, that's okay. It's normal. Remember, the Bible is a spiritual book, written by a spiritual being for spiritual beings. If you don't understand everything, welcome to the club! I'm writing to you not as a seasoned theologian, but as a fellow kindergartner reader. There is always more to be learned and understood in the Bible and the words of God. I love talking to my parents and mentors about what God is teaching them through the Bible. All have walked in Christ before me for many years, studying the Bible and its teachings, and today they're still learning. God continues to reveal insights to their hearts.

But like a kindergartner trying to learn their ABCs or 1-2-3s, we need a simple and practical way to begin to engrain these teachings on our hearts. If we really want to see our relationships get better, and want to love with a genuine, true, and real love, then we need to start memorizing Scripture.

My friend Zach was at a crossroads during what was supposed to be the greatest time in his life. Zach and I were just weeks away from graduating. We were so close to graduation, in fact, that I was in the middle of studying for finals in my dorm room when I heard a knock on the door.

"Hey, Michael, you in there?" asked Zach.

I opened the door. "Hey, Zach, what's going on?"

"You want to go grab some dinner?" Zach asked.

Thinking that there must be something up, I grabbed my jacket, dropped what I was doing, and walked with him across the street to our favorite Chinese restaurant. Being open 24/7, it was a hot spot for starving college kids in the early morning hours.

As we talked about finals and graduation plans, Zach stopped me dead in my tracks.

"Michael, my parents are getting a divorce," Zach said, trying to hold back tears.

My heart broke for Zach. Here we were in college, on the threshold of transitioning into life on our own as adults, and he was faced with this heavy trial.

"Zach, I am so sorry, dude," I said. "I can't imagine what you must be feeling."

Zach then started sharing with me that he had known

this was coming for a long time. He shared that his parents' relationship hadn't been good for years. He told me that he thought they were going to wait until after he had graduated to make this decision. But he wasn't surprised they couldn't make it that long.

"I wanted to ask if you could give me some advice," Zach said. "Isn't your grandpa that well-respected marriage and family expert? What do you think I should do?"

I stared down at my plate of Springfield-style cashew chicken and instantly thought of the verses that my grandfather and I learned when I was a ten-year-old. The memories flooded back.

"Zach, how would you like to be healed of this pain you're feeling, and how would you like to break free of the curse of divorce from the pain caused by your family?" I asked.

Zach instantly lit up with excitement. "Yes!" he said. "I want that really bad."

I quickly flagged down our waiter and asked for a pen and paper.

"Zach, are you ready to make the most important decision of your life?" I asked.

"What do you mean?" Zach replied.

I began telling him my story of the transformative power of God's Word in my life, and how it changed me from the inside out. I told him that it broke the bonds of anger, depression, and low self-esteem, and even changed my relationships.

"Michael, I need this," Zach said.

Over the next several weeks, Zach and I began memorizing Scripture together. Whether in class or during his free time, Zach digested each of these verses together with me, repeating them over and over:

- **Matthew 5:3:** "You're blessed when you're at the end of your rope. With less of you there is more of God and his rule." (MSG)
- **Mark 12:30–31:** "'And you shall love the Lord your God with all your heart and with all your soul and with all your mind and with all your strength.'... 'You shall love your neighbor as yourself.' There is no other commandment greater than these." (ESV)
- **Hebrews 12:10:** "Be devoted to one another in love. Honor one another above yourselves." (NIV)
- **Matthew 5:10–12:** "God blesses those who are persecuted for doing right, for the Kingdom of Heaven is theirs. God blesses you when people mock you and persecute you and lie about you and say all sorts of evil things against you because you are my followers. Be happy about it! Be very glad! For a great reward awaits you in heaven. And remember, the ancient prophets were persecuted in the same way." (NLT)

From that moment on, something changed in Zach. He honored his mom and dad through their divorce; he was there for his little brother, who also was going through a rough patch; and today he's in a healthy relationship with a beautiful woman who is deeply and madly in love with him. With the help of God, and the right tools obtained from His toolbox by reading and memorizing Scripture, Zach had a complete life change.

Seeing Zach walk confidently across the stage to get his diploma meant the world to me. He said his life had been changed forever, and though he didn't have a healthy relationship modeled for him, he was leaning into and trusting in God to make something new through him.

IT BEGINS WITH THE HEART

The change in Zach's life is inspiring. I'm not sure there's anyone who hears a testimony of the transformative power of Jesus' words and says, "Nah, I'm good." But after you start memorizing Scripture, it's important to keep a vital part of this process in mind. Relationships are about the *heart*, not the mind. While the words of Christ are alive and sharper than a two-edged sword, it's not the very words that change you. It's Jesus Christ who changes you.

By reading Scripture and memorizing its words, Zach was allowing the Holy Spirit to do a mighty work in him. It wasn't the ink on the page that was changing him, otherwise all we'd have to do is look at or touch the Bible to be instantly healed. It's so much more complex than that. God was transforming Zach's heart by making it more like His heart. Remember, by reading God's Word, you are entering into a relationship with Him. You are expressing His love language and allowing Him to be in relationship with you. Listen to what Jesus says about this process:

> Why are you so polite with me, always saying "Yes, sir," and "That's right, sir," but never doing a thing I tell you? These words I speak to you are not mere additions to your life, homeowner improvements to your standard of living. They are foundation words, words to build a life on. If you work the words into your life, you are like a smart carpenter who dug deep and laid the foundation of his house on bedrock. When the river burst its banks and crashed against the house, nothing could shake it; it was built to last. But if you just use my words in Bible studies and don't work them into your life, you are like a dumb carpenter who built a house but skipped the foundation. When the swollen river came crashing in, it collapsed like a house of cards. It was a total loss. (Luke 6:46–48)

When I want to fix a leak in my house, I don't want to use duct tape. While duct tape is a solid temporary solution and may for a while stop water from completely soaking my bathroom, it won't fix the problem permanently. It becomes less sticky. And water begins to disintegrate the materials that hold it together. The next time I turn on the faucet and leave it on for just a short while, water seeps through the weaknesses and bursts through the seams. I'm stuck with a puddle of water once again.

But if I want a true fix, I invite a plumber over to take a look. The plumber is much more equipped to find the weakness in the pipe and discover where the leak is coming from. He then sifts through his box of tools, wrenches, and various piping, and figures out the best fit for my sink. Then he starts to do his work. Removing the old pipe, he replaces it with something new. My pipe goes from a sad, leaky mess to something sparkling, solid, and leak-free.

If we follow Jesus' encouragement to be a smart carpenter, building our foundation for life on His words, instead of a dumb carpenter who skips the foundation, our house will stand its ground when the waters blast around it. Like a good carpenter or plumber, God has the power to seek out where our troubles lie and has the tools necessary to fix our foundation or the tough-to-spot leak. He then repairs it with the right specialized tools and makes it new. "The old has passed away; behold, the new has come" (2 Cor. 5:17 ESV). It's the difference between bedrock and a quick fix.

CHANGE OF HEART, NOT BEHAVIOR

As Christians, we have the tendency to become managers of our sin. It's kind of like a badly managed office. Instead of firing bad employees who continue to stab you in the back or lose all of your money, you just redirect them into a different department. You think that by putting them in the basement, where they are out of sight and out of mind, you've eliminated the problem. But just because you can't see them every day at the water cooler doesn't mean they don't still have access to the bank accounts and your internal servers. They continue to wreak havoc even in the shadows. Shoving our sin into the depths of our heart and pretending it's not there is a dangerous trap for Christians. It's called behavior modification.

We can never get rid of our sin fully without the transformative power of God. And one of the most direct accesses we have to this power is through His Word. I'm not saying that God does miracles only through His Word. He has the power and supernatural understanding to do miracles no matter what. But His Word is a proven and powerful way to get in front of the King.

By your words I can see where I'm going;
they throw a beam of light on my dark path.
I've committed myself and I'll never turn back
from living by your righteous order.
Everything's falling apart on me, God;
put me together again with your Word.
Festoon me with your finest sayings, God;
teach me your holy rules. (Psalm 119:105)

Imagine having access 24/7 to the president of the United States. Imagine that you have a direct line to the Oval Office, and the president is guaranteed to take your call. In fact, he is so excited about your call that he is completely focused on and engaged with your words. He wants to be in relationship with you and, because of this, is willing to help you with whatever means necessary. That's what we have, but with the King of the Universe! "But if you remain in me and my words remain in you, you may ask for anything you want, and it will be granted!" (John 15:7 NLT).

You won't be transformed until God transforms your heart. That's the reason we write the Word of God on our hearts. Because by these words, we are given more of His love. Without God's Word, you can try to get rid of that pornography addiction by yourself. You can put blocks on your computer or recruit an accountability partner, but you can never fully rid yourself of it. The ugliness of sin will break free through another weakness. And you'll relapse.

If you're a serial cheater in your relationships, you'll always be a cheater, shortchanging your partner at every opportunity. Even if you don't physically enter into a relationship with someone else while you're dating or married, you may always silently compare what you have, thinking the grass just might be greener on the other side.

Sin is just a fancy word for strongholds in your heart laid down by Satan. Every time you mess up, he's there to lay more bricks. Every time you think a bad thought, more bricks. You start to veer off course by just one degree, more bricks. But through God's Word, you can swing a wrecking ball toward the strongholds and turn them to dust. You are not a slave to evil, but an active participant in victory.

What we're after is heart transformation, not behavior modification. The fairytale is sin management; the truth is God's reconstructive abilities through His Word. Memorizing the Word is a great way to get yourself engaged and on the field. But heart transformation is the home run. When you open your heart to God's powerful Word, He opens you up and does open heart surgery on you. No matter what you're going through, no matter what difficulty you can't seem to overcome with God's help, it isn't permanent; it's temporary.

MORE OF HIS LOVE

The secret to real life love is intertwined with a real life Savior. When it is all said and done, Jesus is the greatest giver of love. Love doesn't just spring out of nowhere. Love isn't secreted by an organ in our body. We don't have a "love muscle" or "love spleen." We cannot create love. It doesn't come from a pill or magical potion. It comes from God alone.

That's why memorizing and meditating on His Word is so important if we're going to have healthy relationships. That's what it's there for. The Word isn't just another folktale; it's not just a compelling story; it's an autobiography from God. This is why we're encouraged not to just keep His commands. That's behavior modification. A chimpanzee knows how to follow commands. But we're called to write them on our heart:

My son, keep my words
and treasure up my commandments with you;
keep my commandments and live;
keep my teaching as the apple of your eye;
bind them on your fingers;
write them on the tablet of your heart. (Proverbs 7:1–3 ESV)

Remember those cheesy commercials from local furniture stores? The ones where the owner of the store would say things like "You want green chairs? We got them!" or "You want king-sized beds for half off? We got them!" While those commercials were in desperate need of a zap of excitement and originality, they bring up a great point. There are so many people facing so many things when it comes to love: broken hearts, addictions, painful pasts, distrust, affairs, abuse. The list goes on and on.

But God, on His glorious throne in heaven, sees each one and is shouting, "Do you need deliverance from porn? I got it!" or "Do you need deliverance from an abusive past? I got that too!" He is calling for you to swallow your pride, stop making excuses, and begin a relationship with Him. No purchase necessary. Because that's when He begins to help you enter into real relationships with others. What do you have to lose?

As you start diving into the Word, it's important to have a battle plan to approach reading Scripture. Here's one that has really helped me have intentional time with Jesus, and that can give Him the open door to begin transforming your heart:

Read: Obviously, this is an important element. Don't just inhale the words quickly. As you read, take your time and try your best to understand each word.

Emotion: The Bible is an emotional book. Emotion is a gateway for the Holy Spirit. Try to grasp each emotion of the particular passage you're diving into. Is it joyous? Is it sad? Are the characters shouting out in praise? Or are they lamenting in sorrow? Put yourself in the book and feel all the feelings.

Discovery: After you're finished reading, take a second to pause and ask the Lord what He is trying to reveal to you. Start thanking Him for the things He was teaching the people in the Bible and ask Him to begin to transform your heart in those same ways.

Recap: I have fallen in love with commentaries. One of my favorites is the *Fire Bible,* produced by the Assemblies of God. In a Bible with commentaries, a theologian or biblical scholar offers their take on what's happening in the Scripture. These men and women immerse themselves in Scripture and are masters of reading between the lines to understand it better. Believe me, they will help you understand it better too. Consider purchasing a commentary to have on hand, in addition to your Bible.

I can't wait for you to see how God is going to trans-form you through His Word. To watch it change the way you think, pray, communicate, and love. Like the ripples made by throwing a rock into a still pond, the ripples from this new decision will make their way to every shore in your life.

Including in the way you love.

PART 3

Growing in Love
for Others

CHAPTER 6

Servanthood

*Real life love is all about service
rather than satisfaction.*

You are a servant. Let that soak in for a second. For some, including myself, it is a tough pill to swallow. You live a life that is not your own. And whether you like it or not, your time on earth is not just your own either.

Our culture tries its best to help us forget that simple fact. Each and every day, we are bombarded with messages and opportunities to make life about "me." Don't believe it? Just turn on any television network and watch one show for an hour. You'll probably see a story line in which a character is pursuing some sort of self-interest. Maybe a romantic relationship or job opportunity. Maybe it's a sinister plot, good versus evil, or a lighthearted rom-com. No matter what, there is always self-interest embedded.

Now take a look at the commercials. How many restaurant advertisements do you count? How many alcohol commercials? What about beauty products? How about medications? How many times have you heard the phrase "You deserve it!"? From facial ads to car ads, everyone is trying to profit off of making you believe that you're the center of your world. Let's face it. We are trapped in a way of thinking that puts "me" at the center of the world.

And it's trickled into pretty much every part of our life. Think about your goals. What do you want to achieve? Do they benefit just you? Or do they help someone else?

What about your relationships? Are you friends with that person just because they can help open up doors for you? Do they give you special status? Are you seeing someone simply because they have a lot of money? While these questions seem a bit unsettling, it brings up an important question: Do you live in a "me"-only culture?

SERVE TO LOVE?

Our society hates the idea of servanthood. And for good reason. Servanthood often brings up painful memories of slavery in American history, as well as in the history of many other countries around the world. Not to mention the reason we crossed the Atlantic, and set up shop in America, away from British rule. We squirm at the idea of our life not being our own and of allowing others to be in control of us in any way. And even more so if our interests would be second, not first. Our identity as a free people of the world is rooted in the idea that freedom is our greatest gift—freedom to do what we want, act the way we want, worship the way we want, and love who we want.

But while these liberties are in fact a gift from God and some of the most important things we possess as humans, when it comes to our relationships and having real love in our life, we have to play by a different set of rules. Real life love is not about you. It has everything to do with others. Real life love is all about service rather than satisfaction.

As scandalous as this idea of living a life of servanthood is today, it was even more so two thousand years ago when Jesus walked the earth. Even His disciples couldn't fully grasp this foreign concept.

When the other ten heard of this conversation, they lost their tempers with James and John. Jesus got them together to settle things down. "You've observed how godless rulers throw their weight around," he said, "and when people get a little power how quickly it goes to their heads. It's not going to be that way with you. Whoever wants to be great must become a *servant*. Whoever wants to be first among you must be your *slave*. That is what the Son of Man has done: He came to serve, not to be served—and then to give away his life in exchange for many who are held hostage. (Mark 10:43–45, emphasis added)

Servanthood? Slavery? Is that all it takes, Jesus? Nothing about that statement seems appealing. But in reality, it's the key that unlocks the door to great relationships.

While the idea of being a servant is scary, let me ease your mind. Servanthood and the slavery Jesus is referring to are simply the act of putting others first. Servanthood says, *You are so valuable to me, that I want to put you and your interests over mine.* The word *me* doesn't exist in a servant's vocabulary. True servanthood doesn't come with bondage, oppression, or anger. It brings deeper love, intimacy, peace, and harmony. In fact, by choosing to be a servant, we actually become more free.

It is absolutely clear that God has called you to a free life. Just make sure that you don't use this freedom as an excuse to do whatever you want to do and destroy your freedom. Rather, use your freedom to *serve* one another in love; that's how freedom grows. For everything we know about God's Word is summed up in a single sentence: Love others as you love yourself. That's an act of true freedom. (Galatians 5:13, emphasis added)

One of my favorite examples of servanthood is from the show *Downton Abbey*. Sure, make all the jokes and jabs you want, but that show was a quality piece of television. If you're not familiar, you should binge-watch all six seasons. Don't knock it until you try it!

To save time, let me quickly summarize the show for you. The story follows two very different worlds. The lives of the wealthy Crawley family, who live like royalty in a great house; and the lives of the servants who live along-side of them. Together, these worlds collide in more ways than one and create a fantastic drama. But more than with the drama, I was always so impressed by the fact that these servants, serving the "family upstairs," give their lives to improving the lives of others. They serve the Crawley family with love, devotion, and oftentimes without complaint. Each is faithful in their service. And they grow to love the members of the family as their own. As someone who struggles with just the idea of helping out around the house when I have something else "more important" on my agenda, I can't imagine centering my life around service. Let alone serving other humans. But Jesus commands us to do so.

None of us are above servanthood. And if you think you are, I have one question for you: *Are you above Jesus?* Being a servant is an important element in the formula for truly loving people, because the greatest act of love in the history of the universe occurred as a loving act toward us. God sent His son Jesus down to earth to live a perfect life and die on the Cross. Christ came to be a servant, giving the ultimate sacrifice and the ultimate act of love: "For even the Son of Man came not to be served but to serve, and to give his life as a ransom for many" (Mark 10:45 ESV).

Luckily, chances are you won't be called to make the ultimate sacrifice of love by giving your life in service to someone. Though people do. Like the great men and women of our armed forces. But you are called every day to give up yourself—your plans, your agenda, your well-being—for the people you love.

PLANTING SEEDS

Farming in the ancient world was a servant's job. Back then, people didn't have the luxury of grocery stores filled with shelf after shelf of food. There wasn't McDonald's. You didn't have Uber Eats, and not only were there no pizza delivery places, there wasn't even pizza.

Everything that went into your mouth was raised by you or your neighbors. The vegetables, fruits, nuts, seeds, and even the animals used for meat were most likely raised in your backyard. And if you weren't wealthy, you were the one taking care of this process. It was your responsibility to work the land, planting seeds that would hopefully grow up into fruitful crops.

Your entire life revolved around the harvest. Quite literally. If your fields yielded a great harvest, you were going to have a great winter. But if you planted seeds in all the wrong places or planted earlier or later than you should have, you were going to starve. In many cases, those whose fields didn't yield a harvest didn't make it to see another winter.

Just like it did in ancient Israel, planting still exists today. Though the majority of us don't have to tend physical fields anymore and instead have the luxury of grocery stores and fast food, we still continue to plant seeds. But we plant different kinds of seeds: seeds of servanthood. Jesus alluded to this process with one of His many parables.

> Listen. What do you make of this? A farmer planted seed. As he scattered the seed, some of it fell on the road and birds ate it. Some fell in the gravel; it sprouted quickly but didn't put down roots, so when the sun came up it withered just as quickly. Some fell in the weeds; as it came up, it was strangled among the weeds and nothing came of it. Some fell on good earth and came up with a flourish, producing a harvest exceeding his wildest dreams. (Mark 4:3–8)

Every act of serving someone is planted in the garden of your relationship with that person as a seed. Over time, that seed sprouts out of the ground and turns into a beautiful tree bearing delicious and bountiful fruit. Each and every day, we plant seeds in the ground with the people we love. We do this through acts of service. Some seeds never fully take root; others deeply embed themselves in the ground. When we do things like take the garbage out on a cold wintry day, that's planting a seed of service. Going out to coffee and listening to a friend share the struggles of his heart is planting a seed. Bringing your girlfriend her favorite drink on a hard day is planting a seed. Or maybe you decide to give above and beyond your tithe and offerings by giving to missions? That's planting more seeds.

Each one of those seeds is planted into the soil of our hearts and in the hearts of those we serve. Those seeds have the potential to help you grow into deeper love for that person.

But much like the farmers of old, we have a choice. We can choose to be wise about when we plant seeds and what seeds we plant. We can tend the soil and give our seeds the best chance to yield a great harvest. Or we can choose the opposite. Instead of being intentional about planting our seeds, we can be brash. We can throw some seeds here and there, hoping something takes root. We can let the soil become dry and dusty. We can skip plowing. And we can choose to plant crops that we're not sure will really take root. But just like in any harvest, in both scenarios we reap what we sow.

If we want to reap a good harvest, we have to sow good seeds. And before we can plant good seeds, we have to know what those seeds are. When we sow good seeds, or intentional acts of service, we're really asking three questions:

1. Why do I serve?
2. How do I serve?
3. When do I serve?

Just like the *Farmer's Almanac*, which helps us figure out when to plant seed and what seed to plant, these three questions are a great tool to use when we desire to serve the people in our life. They help us gauge where our heart is. In each of our decisions to serve, there are always two different motivations. The first motivation we serve is expressing His love, which then helps strengthen our love. Or we serve to benefit ourselves. Which has no benefits for love. In fact, it sucks out our love like a gas thief siphons out a car's gas. One makes relationships soar. The other is the reason they stall out.

WHY DO I SERVE?

When we ask, *Why do I serve?* we're really asking, *What is my motivation behind this act of service?* There are so many reasons for serving someone. Many people engage in some act of service because they think of it as a transactional experience. As if service is like a credit card with cash back or airline miles perks, we think that if we swipe our card by serving someone, we're automatically entitled to get something back. Maybe that person will help us in our time of need. Or maybe they will give to our cause when we call on them. In this deadly way of thinking, we aren't servants at all. We become tax collectors, looking for every opportunity to collect what we're owed and serve ourselves. In fact, we actually turn the person we're serving into our servant.

When we serve someone specifically for our benefit or gain, we end up trying to pull a fast one on God. We try to act like we're doing something good and hope to receive the love God promises us when we "love" others through serving them. But our love comes with a cost because we then expect something in return. When we serve for any reason besides demonstrating love, God hates it.

Remember the parable of the unforgiving servant? In case you don't, let me jog your memory. Jesus tells this story of a servant who owed mountains of debt to his master. It was collection time. Because the servant didn't have the money he owed, the master was going to sell him and his wife and their kids to settle the debt. The servant begged and begged for forgiveness of his loans. After hearing his plea, the master forgave the man of all his debts. Instead of celebrating this great gift, the servant then immediately turned around and saw one of his fellow servants, who owed him just a few pieces of silver. When that man didn't have what he owed, the servant threw him in jail. When his master heard about this, he was outraged. And then the master had the wicked servant thrown into prison to be tortured until he could pay back what he owed.

This sobering parable makes us look at ourselves. Are we serving just to get off the hook with God or get more from God, then turning around and expecting something in return from the people we're serving? Or are we serving with a cheerful heart, ready and eager to go out of our way to help the people we love? Are we a wicked servant or a faithful servant?

I have fallen into the trap of turning my service into transactions. When I was in high school, all I wanted to do was make a ton of money. Even now, it's a mindset that I have to work hard to fight against. Back then, everything I wanted to do in life resulted in one person benefiting: me.

One of my big dreams was to move to Hollywood to become the next Ryan Seacrest. Let's face it: Ryan has the good life. He jets around the world, lives in a gorgeous home in Beverly Hills, dates the prettiest women, and gets to sit by Kelly Ripa and hobnob with famous movie stars on their talk show. Who wouldn't want that life?

Whenever I would share these dreams with my grandfather, he would always ask me:

How does being the next Ryan Seacrest serve people?

How does this move the needle in helping people become the best versions of themselves?

How does this dream help others accomplish their dreams?

Each time he asked me that, I would try to come up with some reason. I tried everything from *I would help the designers of luxury cars by purchasing one of their vehicles with all the money I'd make* to *I'd make sure to promote recycling on my national television show*. But after I began thinking it through, I realized quickly that my intentions were all self-absorbed and that I wouldn't be doing what Christ commands us to do: "Each of you should use whatever gift you have received to serve others, as faithful stewards of God's grace in its various forms" (1 Pet. 4:10 NIV).

That's the real reason we serve. Servanthood recognizes the gift Christ gave us by dying on the Cross and copycats that love to other people. When we serve from the right frame of mind, all we desire is to help people just as Christ helped us. Real life love is born out of that mentality. Serving people in the same way Christ served us shatters the fairytale, that Rick Warren alluded to in a blog post, that we're put on this earth to make a lot of money, retire, be comfortable, and die. Our hearts burn for something more. That's why we serve.

<h2 style="text-align:center">HOW DO I SERVE?</h2>

Once you understand the importance of your motivation to serve, the actual act of service is the easy part. Acts of service are limited solely by your imagination. They can be as big as moving to Africa and adopting thirteen kids, or as small as smiling at someone who looks like they're having a rough day. Servanthood is about expressing God's love. And the rest just falls into place.

Acts of service always fall into two different categories: You either give your *time* or you give your *money*. And as it so happens, our time and money are some of the most precious things we have. Because we have only so much. Even if you have billions of dollars in the bank, you still have only that much. There's still a point where you can reach a zero-dollar balance. And we have only so much time here on this earth. At some point, we're going to pass on into eternity. For many of us, the idea of giving up our time or our money or both is scary. But once you make the decision, you'll find you can't lose.

When looking at how we serve within our relationships, we must first look at the person we're serving. The way that I desire to be served is more than likely different from how you want to be served. For example, when someone takes the time to help me in a specific way, I feel the most loved. Cooking my favorite dinner after I've had a tough day, surprising me by having my car cleaned out when I've been too swamped at work to do it myself, or helping out with my responsibilities around the house: These random acts of service by my friends, family, and roommates make a huge difference for me. And I can feel love bubble up within me, which then helps us grow closer together.

But that's just me. We all carry our own language of service. And it's up to us to discover what that is. Just as we all have ways we like to be loved (like those outlined in Dr. Gary Chapman's book *The 5 Love Languages*), we all desire to be served in a specific way, either with time or with money. The best way to discover what kind of service people you're in relationship with want is to simply ask. It's not going to shut the person down; in fact, it's an honoring question to ask. Maybe they're a time person like me and ask that you give one hour each day, or one hour each week, to lighten their load in some way—like cleaning up the kitchen, doing an errand that's all the way across town, taking on an extra project at work, or just being available to chat over a cup of coffee.

If it's not time, maybe they feel the most served through money. That's not a superficial language of service; it just means that they need that financial investment to feel the most served. If you ask these folks what they need, you might hear answers like purchasing little gifts that remind you of them, delivering a cup of their favorite coffee to their work, surprising them by filling up their gas tank, purchasing them a new outfit, or taking them out to lunch or a nice dinner.

Here's a short test you can take that might help you know how you like to be served. For each pair of statements, circle the A or B beside the one that best describes you. Then add up how many of each letter you scored to see which is higher:

How May I Serve You?

A My ideal day is spent with someone by my side.

B Gifts make me feel appreciated.

A I like it when someone offers to lighten my schedule.

B Coffee or my favorite snack on a hard day immediately brightens it.

A If you want to make me feel loved, clean my living space.

B Give me something that reminds you of me, and I'll give you my heart.

A I have the most fun when someone does a fun activity with me.

B I love receiving gift cards to my favorite restaurants and activities.

A One-on-one time is my favorite time.

B I love being taken shopping for a new outfit or item.

> **A** My favorite birthday memory is of when someone took me on a fun adventure.
>
> **B** My favorite birthday memory is of when I received my favorite and most expensive present of all time.
>
> **A** The best dates are when we just stay at home and make a fun dinner together.
>
> **B** The best dates are when someone takes me out to a nice dinner at my favorite restaurant.
>
> **A** My favorite part of a concert is being there with you.
>
> **B** My favorite part of a concert is our great seats and getting the band's T-shirt.
>
> **A** Forget getting me a card to tell me you love me! I just want you to take me somewhere fun.
>
> **B** Neglecting to get me a card on our special day would be a big mistake.
>
> **A** Taking the time to clean the kitchen for me means the world.
>
> **B** Booking a cleaning service to clean my house? Yes!
>
> _____ **Total As**
>
> _____ **Total Bs**

My grandpa was the master of discovering the way people liked to be served. For example, when my sister Hannah was growing up, Grandpa used to take her to Target on their weekly date. He would sit in the Barbie section for hours upon hours as she decided whether to get the Barbie Malibu set or the Barbie Jet Plane set. Hannah, to this day, likes to be served with a financial investment.

With me, Grandpa used to take me on speaking trips—trips when Grandpa was invited to speak somewhere. We traveled all over the world together. In fact, it was on these trips that I received much of the wisdom you've been reading in this book. We would sit at a cool restaurant for hours, and I would ask him questions, and he would teach me. He understood that serving with his time was important to me.

How do you like to be served? If you answered with mostly As, then you like to be served by people giving you their time. If you answered with mostly Bs, you most like to be served through a financial investment.

However you prefer to be served, you still need to invest in others by serving them how they like to be served. That investment turns into a seed, which, if it takes root, turns into a deeper relationship. Servanthood is the quickest way to relational harmony.

We hear all the time how important it is to do self-care. Our relationships need relational care. Just like we need to get away and do what helps us recharge our batteries, we also need to recharge our relationships. By serving others, your relationships with them get a refresh and grow in energy and freedom, which in turn helps you too.

It's true. Serving others can give you some great health

benefits. Scientists recently conducted a study that mea-
sured how our bodies react to random acts of kindness.
Some were as simple as letting the person behind you go
in front at the grocery store. They found that these acts of
kindness produce serotonin in our brain, causing feelings
of calmness and even helping heal wounds. A Berkeley
study found something similar: It discovered that 50 percent of its participants reported feeling stronger and having
more energy after helping others, with reports of greater
feelings of calmness and enhanced self-esteem.

I'll admit, I thought that was maybe a little too good to
be true. I mean, could servanthood really do all of that for
me? Knowing that this chapter would be included in this
book, I decided to put this theory to the test. I just looked
for someone in need and a way I could go above and beyond
to serve them. Soon I found my targets.

My friends Marcus and Shannon have been in the middle of a stressful and long-drawn-out adoption. Beyond the
stress of bringing a new child into their home, they also
both work full-time jobs and are successful at what they do.
Both Marcus and Shannon have been there for me in more
ways than one. Inviting me over for family dinners, taking me to lunch after church on Sundays, and practically
adopting me into their family, this couple has served me
with both their time and money. So I wanted to do something in return to reciprocate their kindness.

One evening while I was driving down the freeway
in the town where we live, Marcus called me. He told

me they'd gotten a grim update on the adoption of their son and their adoption date had been pushed back several more weeks, maybe even months. I could hear their young son laughing and playing in the background, and Marcus mentioned that Shannon wouldn't be home for a while.

It hit me. Shannon once told me that an easy way to serve people is through food. Passing their exit on the freeway, I asked Marcus what their dinner plans were. He said he was most likely going to grab another take-out meal. I told him to cancel those plans, because they were having a home-cooked meal.

"From who?" he asked.

"Me!" I said.

Marcus seemed excited with a hint of disbelief that I was actually going to cook. He told me to come on over. So I canceled my plans, stopped at the grocery store, and picked up some ingredients for a meal that was one of my favorites: my mom's poppy-seed chicken casserole. If that couldn't soothe the heart, I didn't know what could.

Honestly, my heart instantly felt full. While my test wasn't exactly scientific, to know that I might have lightened their load through a Ritz-Cracker poppy-seed chicken casserole made me feel warm inside, like I was truly making a small difference. Later, when Shannon told me it was a blessing to come home from a long day at work to an already prepared meal, it meant the world.

A few more times during their adoption process, I called Marcus and said, "Cancel your dinner plans, because I'm coming over!" My rule was, I always did the cooking, and I always paid for the ingredients. It was a simple way to serve some extraordinary friends.

WHEN DO I SERVE?

The timing of when to serve can be difficult for people. I certainly understand why. We're busy. People are busy. Why should I interrupt my life and someone else's life to make a difference? Is it really making a difference anyway?

That is a lie straight from the enemy. We are called to serve others, just like Christ serves us. If we're called to do something, time doesn't matter. There is always time for an act of service. And it's always appreciated, no matter what.

When I was young, my mom taught my sister and me to be spies looking for people who might need help. It's interesting how you catch things that normally are invisible when you're actually looking for them. During summer breaks, my mom would take my sisters and me to Wal-Mart, and we'd sit in the parking lot waiting and watching. If an elderly person was struggling to lift their purchases into their car, my sisters and I would slide open our van's door, investigative-reporting-show–style, and run up to the person to ask how we could help. One day, we hit a record with thirty people. Each one needed assistance in some way. And our rule was: No job is too small or too big. And we never ever accepted a tip. Never. It was just a way we could help.

Imagine how fruitful our relationships would be if we acted as spies in our own environments? In our homes, dorms, places of work, grocery stores, or favorite restaurants? The list goes on and on. All it takes is making the decision to put on your "spy glasses" of service and see what needs to be done. Then you need to make the decision to take action.

I've found myself stuck in the mentality that I have to wait to do something big in order to serve. I look at people like Katie Davis Majors, who moved across the world at the age of eighteen to take in and foster thirteen young girls, saving them from a life of poverty and starvation. She even started a ministry that provides health services and food to over 1,300 families in Uganda. That's the ultimate act of service, right?

While Katie's story is inspiring, and I believe that God is doing and continues to do incredible work through her and her ministry, it's not the only brand of servanthood that exists. Just because you can't move to a third-world country to pursue mission work—heck, just because you don't even have the spare time or finances to go overseas for only a week—doesn't mean that you aren't a team player in this game of servanthood.

There are still people in your life whom you can begin serving today. People around you are begging to be loved and to be served, but they often go unnoticed. When do those people get to be served? The time is now. And that servant is you.

An easy way to ensure that you begin serving is by actually scheduling a time to serve someone each and every day. No matter if it's someone you're super close to, like your spouse or significant other or maybe a best friend or room-mate, or someone who's just a distant acquaintance at work. They still provide a way to increase your love and grow bet-ter relationships. Who knows? That acquaintance could turn into a best friend. You never know the gems that Jesus hides when we demonstrate real life love toward others in our life.

WHAT DO YOU TREASURE?

Have you ever wondered what our hearts look like to God? Jesus says you can tell a lot about a person by the contents of their heart.

I picture my heart as almost like a filing cabinet. When Jesus opens it up and starts thumbing through the contents, what does He see? My prayer is that He sees a man who loves Him deeply. A man who takes His commandment to love others like Christ loves the church seriously. And some-one who cares enough to help a brother out when needed.

The reality is that no one is perfect. There are a few files in my heart that I wish could get "lost." But that's the price for being human. Each and every day, we have one choice: a choice to think like God or think like the enemy. Our brain can't exist in both places. It's not a surf-and-turf entrée. You can't have both the steak and the lobster. You have to choose one.

When we decide to serve, we start to think how God

thinks. And our heart begins to reflect these thoughts. Instead of files that explain over and over where we failed, we begin to see files of where we shared more of God's love. I love how Jesus puts it:

> Don't hoard treasure down here where it gets eaten by moths and corroded by rust or—worse!—stolen by burglars. Stockpile treasure in heaven, where it's safe from moth and rust and burglars. It's obvious, isn't it? The place where your treasure is, is the place you will most want to be, and end up being. (Matthew 6:19–21)

We all have a sleeping giant of love in our hearts just waiting to be released. And servanthood is a sure way to wake it up. Remember when I said that acts of service shouldn't be done for human gratification? While that might be true, you are nonetheless making an investment. As with sowing seeds into the ground, you're going to get only one of two things: nothing or a bountiful tree. And while you might not ever get the chance to eat of its fruit here on earth, just think of what Jesus is preparing for you in heaven. The treasures of this earth wither and fade. But your investments in heaven will last for ever and ever.

Begin renewing the treasures and files of your heart by acts of service, and watch real life love begin to take deep root in your heart.

CHAPTER 7

Understanding Personality

Personality is the DNA of real life love.

Who knew that a cooling fan could cause so much trouble? And who knew that California could be so hot during the summer months?

I'll never forget my first semester in college. It was day one at my dream school. During my first year as a student, I got the chance of a lifetime to attend a small Christian school outside of Santa Barbara, California. Not only was this school known for its gorgeous campus, it also boasted ocean views, fabulous professors, and a great student body. And while this school had it all, it also had something that I still don't recall reading about in the advertising pamphlets. No air conditioning in the dorms.

I like to be cool. Sleeping in hot mugginess is not my cup of tea. My friends growing up called me a polar bear because my preferred room temperature when I sleep is sixty-five degrees Fahrenheit. But Southern California, whether you like it or not, is just a desert disguised with palm trees and fancy restaurants. Sure, the ocean helps. But only if you're swimming in it. On land, it gets toasty warm.

Today my roommate Kevin remains one of my closest friends. But during those first few months, I didn't think we were going to make it. I was sure that our relationship would end in roommate divorce. Because while I like to sleep in arctic conditions, Kevin prefers a more tropical temperature.

To Kevin, sleeping in the cold is sleeping in seventy-five degrees. Which to me is like sleeping in the Sahara Desert. But as a California native, Kevin loved the hot days. To him they meant more surfing and more comfortable nights. For me they were like sleeping on the surface of the sun. Can you see where there might have been some conflict?

One day, after another sweaty, uncomfortable night, one of my suitemates (we lived with two other guys on our floor) must have overheard my sleeping woes, because he brought in a cooling fan that he wasn't using.

Each night after Kevin fell asleep, I'd get up and turn on the fan. Swinging back and forth, this fan was my saving grace. It cooled down the entire room in seconds. And made my air conditioning–less room more tolerable. But not long after falling asleep, I'd wake up to find myself sweating again—and my fan turned off.

That's weird, I'd think. *It must have come unplugged when Kevin went to the bathroom.*

I was amazed Kevin didn't die from tripping on the cord. Because night after night, my fan would turn off in the wee hours of the morning. For no apparent reason.

After about a week, Kevin came into the room. He looked upset.

"Hey, Kev!" I asked. "What's up?"

"You really want to know?" he asked.

"Yeah, what's up?"

"You've got to do something about that fan. It's freezing me out at night and drying my throat and eyes. So it's out of here."

"But I like the fan," I said.

"Well, I really don't."

Suddenly, Kevin decided to take matters into his own hands and began to carry the fan out. We got into an argument. I was lobbying hard for a fan. Kevin was lobbying hard for our dorm room to stay like a sauna. Back and forth we went. Little did we know that the issue wasn't the fan at all. It was a phenomenon called personality.

SHINING THE SPOTLIGHT ON PERSONALITY

Personality is one of my favorite subjects. I'm not alone. Millions of people have put their personality to the test by taking one of the dozens of BuzzFeed personality quizzes. In fact, 20 million people have taken BuzzFeed's "What City Should You Live In?" quiz alone. That's a lot of people wanting to discover more about who they are and what makes them tick.

But that just scratches the surface of the variety of

personality assessments online. I've seen everything from "What the Starbucks Drink You Like Says About Your Personality" to "Which Punk Icon Are You?" and even "Which Soul-Crushing, Existential Waste of Time on the Internet Are You?" What does this tell us? People are fascinated by what makes them them. And for good reason. Each of us is made up from a complex blueprint that was hand designed by God.

> . . . You shaped me first inside, then out;
> you formed me in my mother's womb.
> I thank you, High God—you're breathtaking!
> Body and soul, I am marvelously made!
> I worship in adoration—what a creation!
> You know me inside and out,
> you know every bone in my body;
> You know exactly how I was made, bit by bit,
> how I was sculpted from nothing into something. (Psalm 139:13–15)

God instilled into each of us a special personality that is unique and designed only for us. As unique as a famous painting, your personality fits you in a way that's second to none. Just think, there was never anyone like you, and there will never be anyone like you again. That's something to be excited and motivated about!

But here's the thing about having 7 billion people all sharing one planet and all with different personalities. Some of us are bound to clash. Not due to a problem, but because of who we are on the inside.

After my first roommate tussle, I tried to think of what the issue could be. I mean, he has blankets? Was my insensitivity really that bad? Then it dawned on me: Kevin's executive decision bothered me. And my passive-aggressive behavior, putting the fan back in our room and on his side, probably bothered him too. As I began thinking about our tiff, I remembered a book my grandpa wrote with his colleague Dr. John Trent when I was a kid called *The Treasure Tree*.

The book follows the story of how a lion, otter, beaver, and golden retriever each figured out how to love one another and work together even though each was so different from the others. Each animal possessed a special trait that helped all of them achieve their goals and navigate their adventures.

I remembered that my personality best matched the golden retriever's. That meant I was more sensitive and tenderhearted. And when provoked or walked over too many times, I have the tendency to bite back. This explained why I was so upset with Kevin and wanted my way.

On the flip side, I realized after recalling my grandpa's book that Kevin's personality matched most with the lion's. He was the very opposite of me. Lions are natural-born leaders and like to take charge. But if not careful, lions have the tendency to bulldoze their way through life, leaving a trail of destruction and hurt feelings.

Both personalities have their weaknesses, but they also contain strengths too. I learned that day that asking Kevin questions instead of challenging his decisions was the best way to confront the misunderstanding. I could best contribute to our friendship by encouraging and bringing laughter. Two of my favorite things.

That night, as I was ready with my new plan of action, Kevin walked into our room. I was standing next to the fan, and Kevin was bracing for all-out World War III. But I had different plans.

"The fan is still here," Kevin said.

"What seems to be the biggest issue with the fan?" I asked.

"Well, it's not the fan necessarily," Kevin said. "It's just that the fan blows a hundred miles an hour all night and it freezes me out."

I continued my questioning by asking how he felt about the fan being at a more mild speed.

"Sure!" he said. "You can keep it on level six or seven. Just not level ten. It feels like a prop plane at that level."

And just like that, our conflict was over. It proved to me that understanding the way people operate opens the door to deeper understanding and empathy. And who knows? You might even discover something else to honor along the way!

A NEW WAY OF LOOKING AT PERSONALITIES

Today I'm still using what I learned in college to help me with how I engage in relationships. Understanding personalities has helped me navigate the crazy world of dating as well as growing up with siblings, honoring my parents, entering the workforce, and working with my peers. Each person I meet is different from the last. But one thing remains the same: We all have unique personalities that make us the way we are.

As silly as my story about living in the dorm is, there's a reason it's stuck in my mind. It was the catalyst for my belief that understanding personality is an important element in our journey toward uncovering the secrets to real life love. Because when you think about all the people you have to deal with, or all the people you will deal with, understanding the way you and others tick will be a great asset to you.

So many of my friends don't get along with their parents, siblings, aunts, uncles, grandparents, bosses, friends, and even sometimes their mate or significant other because they don't understand personalities. The majority of the conflicts people share with me could have been avoided, and even used for their benefit, if they just understood what makes up the other person's personality.

I have avoided many hurt feelings, disappointments, and embarrassments by using a basic understanding of personality. Bridges that should've been burned are today as strong as ever because of this. Personality is the DNA of real life love. Without a basic understanding of who people are, why they do the things they do, and say the things they say, you'll be trying to search for hidden treasure without a map!

As I've grown older, I've searched for the right tool to

gauge personalities. I've searched far and wide for a deeper understanding of the science of myself and others. I've looked through every *Star Wars* character quiz, fast-food-item quiz, ENFP personality test, and anything the Internet had to offer. Each time, I came back with nothing.

Sitting down for dinner with a friend in Seattle, Washington, was when my search ended. Over an Italian meal, Dr. Les Parrott, my friend and mentor, told me about his research and findings on personality. He said that he and a group of researchers had been working hard for decades to uncover and ultimately unpack the unique personalities of people. If anyone was going to crack the code on fully understanding personality, it would be Dr. Parrott.

As a psychologist and best-selling author of over fifty books on relationships, Dr. Parrott and his wife, Leslie, who's also a professor and a marriage and family therapist, have done a lot for helping people discover who they really are and how they love. In fact, Les and Leslie are the cofounders of eHarmony Marriage and worked with Dr. Neil Clark Warren (the grandfatherly gentleman in the eHarmony television commercials) in matching compatible partners online. I'd say their research has worked. More than 600,000 married couples have found each other on the site.

Dr. Parrott couldn't have been more enthusiastic about his latest tool for understanding personality. He calls it the Yada Assessment (*yada* is an ancient Hebrew word that means "to know with your head and your heart"). He told me that instead of using his data and questions to match couples, researchers were now able to plug the data into a set of questions to create a snapshot of who a person is. This new assessment would reveal not only their personality, but their unique fight type, their personal talk style, what they look for in a romantic partner, and even the way they manage time. Embedded in this report was a virtual blueprint of who a person is and how they can become their best self.

I was instantly hooked. Whatever this was that Les had developed, I wanted to get my hands on it. I completed the questionnaire online, and in a matter of seconds, my entire story was laid out in front of me. This was the closest I had ever come to seeing the original blueprints God used to design me. And it was all wrapped up with a bow from a website called Yada.com.

DISSECTING PERSONALITIES

Understanding the way you and others tick is a fun and thrilling task. Somewhere deeply embedded into our DNA is a trait that we all share: wanting to learn more about ourselves and others. Because the more we know about ourselves, the greater the chance that we'll have great relationships.

Before I move on and begin to share with you in greater detail the four main personalities and what makes up each of these special traits, I'd like to encourage you to take the Yada Assessment. It's such a helpful tool and asset for understanding yourself and the way you engage in relationships. The Yada website takes less than fifteen minutes to reveal your results, and it provides you with ten powerful pages of practical information specifically for you. Just go online to MichaelGibson.org and you'll find a link to the Yada Assessment website.

I recommend you do it now.

Seriously. Do it right now, and you'll have your custom report to refer to as we walk through the remainder of this chapter! Of course, you don't *have* to take the assessment to learn about the various personalities I'm about to show you, but it will make them far more meaningful.

By the way, there's a very small fee for the Yada Assessment. Don't let that slow you down. Just consider it an investment in you. And if you go first to my website, MichaelGibson.org, you can find a special promo code that will give you a discount.

So go ahead and take the assessment—you can do it on your phone, tablet, or computer. Then come back to the remainder of this chapter.

Okay, I'm assuming you've now taken the Yada Assessment. You now know a whole lot more about your personality. By the way, those paragraphs on the first page of your report, the ones describing your particular personality—they are unique to you. The Yada Assessment has nearly forty thousand variables that go into what you just read—so you won't see those exact paragraphs on anyone else's Yada Report. Ready to dig in?

TASK-ORIENTED? OR PEOPLE-ORIENTED?

There is a reason why Chick-fil-A sold over $7 billion worth of chicken in 2017. Just to put that into perspective, that's more money than the entire country of Zimbabwe makes in a year.

So why does Chick-fil-A sell so much chicken? Because they have mastered the art of customer service. They're famous for making you feel famous anytime you walk into their restaurant. Chick-fil-A is all about people. It's no wonder that S. Truett Cathy, the founder of Chick-fil-A, often said, "We should be about more than just selling chicken. We should be a part of our customers' lives and the communities in which we serve."

Chick-fil-A is people-oriented. Each of their employees goes above and beyond to make customers feel like royalty. You'll hear a kind "my pleasure" after you say "thanks." And if there's an issue with your food or service, you come first. Always. People over profit. Satisfaction over sales. What they're doing must be working. Because sales increase for Chick-fil-A each year they're in business.

Though Chick-fil-A has mastered the art of caring about people, do you think that each and every employee stands at their counter greeting people with a warm smile? Of course not! At their headquarters in Atlanta, Georgia, there is a group of employees who hardly ever even see a customer their entire careers. Because they're focused on something entirely different from the customer experience. They're focused on the bottom line. They pay attention to each and every business decision and minute detail with precision and meticulousness—everything from the wording on the menu board to the cash registers operating correctly, their food products getting to the correct places and in the correct quantity, their taxes being paid, the cleanliness of the restaurants, and restaurant safety. These are just a few of the other "tasks" at hand that make each restaurant operate.

Chick-fil-A wouldn't have made it this far without looking at both sides: People focused on people, and people focused on tasks. Our world is in a similar boat.

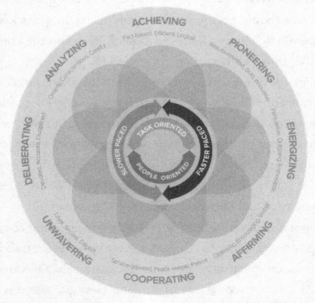

Drs. Les and Leslie Parrott and Yada.com

Research shows that each of us is somewhere between being *people-focused* and *task-focused*—

Task-Oriented

If your personality falls on the top of the pinwheel, then you are considered *task-oriented*. Much like the behind-the-scenes employees at Chick-fil-A, you are focused at getting done what needs to be done. You live your life by a to-do list. In fact, when you wake up, the first thing on your to-do list is to create a to-do list. You strive for accomplishment, and there's nothing that's stopping you from achieving what you want. No matter if it's just a friendly game of one-on-one basketball or an important career position, you want to win. Period. "It's just a game" isn't in your vocabulary. "Second Place Is the First Loser" is your mantra. Getting the job done is top priority. Sometimes even over people's feelings. In fact, if anyone or anything is standing in between you and your goal, it's game time. You put your shoulder down and plow your way to the end zone. You will fight. And you will win. Which is a good thing, because you share a personality trait most commonly found in CEOs, presidents, and world leaders. Without you, nothing would ever get done.

People-Oriented

If your personality falls toward the bottom of the pinwheel, you're more *people-oriented*. People come first. Always. Over your goals. Over your desires. And over the bottom line. You take into consideration the way people feel about something. Brash decisions are a foreign concept to you. When making an important decision, you perform your due diligence to take the temperature of the room and first find out how people feel about the choices. You might find yourself reluctant to speak out if someone's feelings are in jeopardy. If someone has a problem with something or someone, you are quick to find a compromise that everyone is happy with. You are the ultimate team player. If you played in the NBA, you'd lead your team with the most assists. People like you. And you like people.

So which person are you? Are you more focused on the task at hand? Or are you more focused about the well-being of those around you? There isn't a wrong answer here. Each personality type has its wonderful strengths. And each is vitally important. But if you had to choose a team, which one would it be? Here's a chart of words and phrases associated with each that might help you better understand where you fit.

Task-Oriented

Driven

Clearly defined goals

Work from a to-do list

Concentrated and focused

Gets it done now

Intimidating

People-Oriented

Nurturing

Heartfelt connections

Spontaneous

Easily distracted

Procrastinate

Warm and friendly

ARE YOU FAST-PACED OR SLOW-PACED?

Have you ever seen a race between a Porsche 911 and a Toy-ota Prius? One is a hot rod, the other is the more dependable option. Both are great cars. Both will get you from point A to point B, but there is one distinct difference between the two.

If you were to put the Porsche and Prius together on the same racetrack and wave the black-and-white checkered flag, you would probably hear the Porsche's engine revving and its tires peeling out as it thrusts its way into a sure lead. Topping out at more than 198 miles per hour, the Porsche wins the race of speed against the Prius every time. In fact, several times over. Lapping the Prius not just once, but over and over again.

However, if you kept the Porsche at full throttle the entire race, you'd see another phenomenon occur. The Porsche, which runs on gas, will start to shake and slow down to almost a halt. Then, with quiet strength, the Prius will come around the bend, ultimately winning the race with its slow reliability and all-around fuel economy.

Chances are, you probably identify with one of these vehicles. Maybe you live life like the Porsche, lapping your competition at every turn and topping out at more than 198 miles per hour. Or maybe you identify with the Prius.

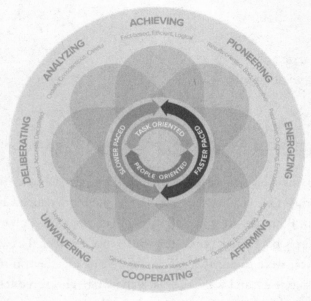

Drs. Les and Leslie Parrott and Yada.com

You live life slowly and methodically. You're intentional with every decision, and you live by the mantra "Slow and Steady Wins the Race."

According to research, your unique personality can be called either fast-paced or slow-paced.

Fast-Paced

If your personality score lies somewhere on the right side of the pinwheel, you are *fast-paced*. You live life in the fast lane. Or even better, in the express lane. Time, and using as little of it as you can to accomplish your tasks, is a big deal for you. You probably catch yourself frequently using the phrases "This is a total waste of time" or "Can't this go any faster?" In fact, not wasting time and getting somewhere the quickest and most efficient way, is extremely important. When carrying in groceries, every finger is assigned to not just one bag but multiple bags. There are no second trips back to the car. Sitting in rush-hour traffic is a nightmare for you. All you can focus on is your dashboard clock counting minute after minute. Your decisions are made as quick as lightning. And they can change in the blink of an eye. And speaking of eyes, you can barely see straight with your jam-packed schedule and constant running to-and-fro. But this gives you energy. In fact, you don't run on regular gasoline, you run on rocket fuel. If someone needs a project done right the first time, and in record speed, you're perfect for the job. Your energy is contagious. And that "get it done" mentality keeps your relationships in tip-top shape.

Slow-Paced

On the other hand, if you are on the left side of the pinwheel, you are *slow-paced*. You take time to smell the roses. Nothing in your life is rushed. Intentionality is your name, and meticulous is your game. You plan out each step carefully and purposefully. Research makes you smile. Spontaneity might make you cringe. When you go to the store to shop for a new sweater, it's an entire experience. You put the shop in *shop*. You take into consideration everything about the sweater. Its brand. The way it feels. How it will wash. Will it last for twenty years? You ask the clerk where it was made. Whether or not the color is really your color. You do your research on where to get the best price possible. And if it's not right, that's okay, you'll find the right one eventually. In short, you are slow-paced.

What do you think? Not sure which category you might fall under? Here's a chart of words and phrases associated with each that might help you make your decision.

Fast-Paced

Divide and conquer

Impatient

Raring to go

To the point

"Don't just sit there! Do something!"

"The early bird catches the worm"

Slow-Paced

Unite and decide

Patient

Take your time

Flowery language

"Think before you act"

"Slow-growing trees bear the best fruit"

Do any of these sound familiar? Do you now see yourself as slow-paced or fast-paced? Or people-oriented or task-oriented? Let's unpack how your unique personality fits into the big picture.

These four important traits are vital to understanding the basis of your personality and what you prefer or don't prefer. I hope this basic explanation of personality and its insight into how people think and reach their decisions helps you understand what makes you tick. For example, if you're more people-oriented, you will go out of your way to help someone in need. If you're in a jam for time but your friend needs a ride to the airport, you are going to go out of your way to try to help. Even if it means being late for your own job, not to mention all the gas money it takes to get them to the airport. People come first for you. And you're going to make sure they get help.

On the flip side, if you are task-oriented, lending a hand to a friend in need depends on your predetermined schedule. Being late to work because of driving your friend to the airport is never going to fly with you. To you, your friend should have been more organized and asked for a ride sooner. Why should you compromise your schedule? To a people-oriented person, this can be frustrating, just as their spontaneity and lack of preparation can be irritating to you. But this isn't a test of kindness or willingness. It's not a display of character either. It's a display of personality. By understanding this in our interactions with people, we're going to better live in harmony.

Similarly, the pace we maintain can put us at odds with one another. If you lean more toward being fast-paced, a boss who takes two weeks just to decide what pens to buy for the office doesn't make a whole lot of sense. But it's just the way they are. They're not hardwired for quick and painless decisions like you are.

On the other hand, if your best friend is always the first one to chime in when you're deciding on a restaurant and likes to make decisions immediately, you might be more than a little irritated as a slow-paced person. It doesn't make any sense to you why your friend doesn't pull out the Yelp app to make an educated decision based on the best reviews. But it's not because they're trying to be domineering or insensitive; it's just who they are.

LEVERAGING YOUR YADA REPORT

Now that you have a sense of what makes up your personality—whether you are fast-paced or slow-paced and whether you are task-oriented or people-oriented—you are ready to take it to the next level. This is especially true if you completed the Yada Assessment and have your Yada Report at the ready.

How? By connecting with others. Now, I can almost feel some of you wincing with anxiety—especially those of you who are more task-oriented. Don't worry, this will be painless. Here's my suggestion. Take the time to share your report with three close friends or family members. They could be your roommate, best friend, parents, siblings, youth pastor, or even a professor you feel comfortable sharing with. Each page will help you explain who you are and how your personality directly correlates to various essential areas of your life, like how you manage your time, communicate with others, handle conflict, and engage in friendships and what you look for in your future spouse.

After I took the Yada Assessment the first time, I was amazed to uncover why I do different things. When I shared my Yada Report with my parents one night over dinner, we laughed for hours about my different quirks and why I have them. For example, I run late. On time for me is fifteen minutes late at least. I take fashionably late very seriously. You can imagine how this has caused frustration for my parents over the years. Late to church. Late to school. Late to parties. I run late.

And together, we were able to uncover why I am this way. Turns out, according to my Yada Report, I am an *improviser* when it comes to managing time. My schedule is easygoing, fluid, and constantly evolving. And I'm people-oriented too. So there's always time for a spontaneous lunch or coffee with a friend, no matter how busy I am.

I'm easily distracted and could make a better effort to set boundaries in place for my appointments and commitments. Once this was out in the open, it clicked for me and my family. Today they know this about me and have started telling me to arrive fifteen minutes before I'm actually supposed to be there. I've been on time ever since! Imagine if the people in your life could instantly understand why you are the way you are! That's the gift of Yada.

Now if you really want to leverage what you learned in this chapter and in your Yada Report, consider starting a small group. Research reveals that one of the best ways to internalize a message so that it makes a lasting difference in your life is to join with about a half dozen other people who are invested in doing the same thing you are. In this case, that's exploring your personalities to learn as much as you can about yourself and how God made you.

Starting a small group is easier than you might guess. And it's low-pressure. You're not signing a contract to meet once a week until you die. In fact, getting together to discuss Yada as a group can last just four or five sessions. If you're wondering what to talk about in your sessions, use the Yada Report as your guide. Here's a four-week track to get you started—

Week 1: Your Personality
Week 2: Your Time Table
Week 3: Your Talk Style
Week 4: Your Fight Type

You certainly don't have to stop after four weeks. This is just the tip of the iceberg. There's also potential for great conversations about how you engage in friendships and even what to look for in finding a spouse someday. The ceiling with Yada is limitless. By the way, in case you're feeling nervous about what to discuss, you'll see that each page of your Yada Report has several discussion starters in its lower right corner highlighted in gray. That's all you need to get going with a small group.

DISCOVERING STORIES

This chapter has taken me the longest to write. I've rewritten it countless times, and spent hours diving into research to better understand this topic. The fact of the matter is, I could have kept going. Personality is like an ocean of knowledge. It's about as complex as things come. And that's good. Because the complexity of the topic shows the incredible complexity we have as humans. Much of what you have read stands on the shoulders of countless years of research by legendary psychologists and brilliant behavioral scientists. While I'm not a scientist or psychologist, personalities still mean a lot to me.

One of the things I've learned from Dr. Les Parrott (whose research is all over this chapter) is that we all have an interesting story to tell. But sometimes we just don't know how to tell it in an interesting way. By understanding the way you tick, and the way others tick, you'll begin to better see why you are the way you are, and why others are the way they are too. The better you understand how your personality shapes the story of your life, the easier it will be for you to experience real life love in your relationships.

The reason I spent more time on personality than any other topic in this book is that I believe in it. I believe in the power of understanding people. You can't lose with this knowledge. Believe me, I've witnessed it firsthand. An understanding of personalities will help you in all your relationships. And they'll help you put into practice the other seven principles we've discussed in this book.

Free to Love

*Don't accept the lie that you are doomed
to a life in which your relationships
really don't mean anything.*

Each one of us copycats the people who taught us how to love. We follow how they learned how to love people, the ways they express love, and even the ways they think about love. They had to come from somewhere. None of us are born with the distinct ability and knowledge of how to love. We learn from the adults in our life, maybe a parent, big brother or sister, grandparent, youth group leader, or even our friends. If you are alive and breathing, then you are the product of someone else's love.

While there are many of us who had good if not great examples of love growing up, there are even more who didn't. Who instead grew up with the idea that God and love don't mix well. They were sold a brand of love that is sick and perverse. A brand of love that is full of lies and fairytales. A love that is of the world and corrupted by human intentions. A love that, if not handled and treated carefully, can rot your soul from the inside out.

THE FAIRYTALE

When you picked up this book and read the cover, I gave you a distinct promise. I promised that if you read the pages of this book, I would help you say goodbye to the fairytale and hello to true relationships. Throughout this book, I've given you all that I've learned so far on this journey of life about how to love well. I showed you seven ways to step out of the shallow tide pools of fake, pretend love and how to jump into an ocean of deep, true, and satisfying relationships. Let's refresh—those seven principles are:

1. **Honor:** loving people and their quirks like the godly creations they are by seeing them as rare bricks of gold.
2. **Anger:** finding and identifying anger in your life and realizing the killing nature of this painful heart disease.
3. **Forgiveness:** releasing anger and acknowledging your own offenses to enter into true peace and harmony with people.
4. **Trials:** learning to celebrate the hard times in life, and how these painful life moments ("oysters") can yield great treasures ("pearls").
5. **God's Word:** recognizing the power of God's Word, a misunderstood love tool, and how the Word of God can transform you and your relationships from the inside out.

6. **Servanthood:** being second in a world of firsts, and seeing yourself as a servant toward God and others to create love in all your relationships.

7. **Understanding People:** learning how to identify and understand people's personalities, and how we are created by God as unique and special.

Each one of these principles is meant to encourage you and help retrain your thinking as to how you should act in relationships. These principles, which I learned growing up as the grandson of Gary Smalley and the son of marriage and family pastors, have been game changers for me.

In these last pages, I've talked a lot about how to increase love in your life. We've talked about the seven secrets to thriving, healthy relationships, which you can begin using today. But after all of this—after you're finished reading, underlining, and taking notes—what is the point? Why care about these seven principles? And why implement them into your life? Would your life really be that different? What is the fairytale you're trying to break out of?

The fairytale is this: that we live in a world that doesn't have a firm definition of what love is. There are millions if not billions of people who get married, have kids, and become grandparents but miss the mark and never fully understand what this thing called "love" really is. The fairytale is believing the lie that dysfunctional, bland, mediocre, and surface-level relationships are really our only option. To me, the most destructive words are "Well, this is about as good as it's going to get with my relationships." What a foreign concept!

The entire point of this book is to show you that you don't have to settle for what the world tells you is true love. Don't believe the lie that you are doomed to a life in which your relationships really don't mean anything. I want to push you to stop being afraid. Real life love doesn't cause fear—it creates faith.

TRUE LOVE COMES FROM JESUS

During my biblical research for this book, I came across a passage in 1 John 4 that wonderfully sums up how we can begin to implement these seven principles. As I was studying this passage, I began to understand the truth of where love comes from. During the writing of the very book you're holding in your hands, I've been learning right along with you. And I discovered where our love comes from: Jesus.

I have had the incredible opportunity to travel to Israel twice. Both times I've gone, the Lord has spoken incredible things to my heart and mind, both while I was there and even in the months and years since I returned home. During my first trip to Israel, I got the opportunity to visit the source of the Jordan River.

The Jordan River is a force of water to be reckoned with. This river is an epicenter of drama all through the Bible. It's the same river that parted when Elijah and Elisha crossed, when Elijah ascended into heaven on chariots of fire, and when Elisha started his ministry. It's the same river in which Jesus was baptized by John the Baptist, when the heavens opened above and the Holy Spirit descended on Him like a dove. This mighty river also feeds the Sea of Galilee, which served as a major backdrop for Jesus' ministry.

This river has seen so much. But if you look at the source of this great river, it isn't as mighty as you'd think. The source is a bubbling spring deep in the heart of Israel, in the Golan Heights. As it moves farther down the mountains, this ever-flowing spring quickly turns into powerful rapids that cut through sharp rocks and then snakes its way through the golden fields of the Armageddon valley and into the Sea of Galilee, finally ending in the Dead Sea.

Just like the spring that creates this powerful river, the spring inside our hearts creates a powerful force of love in our life. It begins deep in the crevices of our hearts. Here's how the disciple John describes the source of our love:

This is how God showed his love for us: God sent his only Son into the world so we might live through him. This is the kind of love we are talking about—not that we once upon a time loved God, but that he loved us and sent his Son as a sacrifice to clear away our sins and the damage they've done to our relationship with God. My dear, dear friends, if God loved us like this, we certainly ought to love each other. No one has seen God, ever. But if we love one another, God dwells deeply within us, and his love becomes complete in us—perfect love! (1 John 3:7–12)

Beginning to implement these keys to create true relationships is really only the start. Things really begin to heat up when God, through His son Jesus, is the source of our love. By choosing to believe in God, and believe that He in His mighty act of love sent His son Jesus down to earth to live a perfect life and take our sin and punishment by dying on the Cross, we are saved. This act by Jesus is the spring of love that bubbles out of our hearts. This is the source that gives us the love that we in turn use toward God, others, and ourselves. In other words, Jesus' act of love is the catalyst of the way we love. When we turn to Jesus, we start to copycat Christ in our acts of love.

Love isn't something that we create ourselves. It's something that God creates for us. He pours it into our hearts and acts in love through us. Jesus shows the people in our life the love that we dream of. And through us, He and only He begins to create a new heart, a heart that exhibits healthy habits like the seven principles in this book.

I want to be very clear as to how you truly transform your life and begin living out real life love. It's not through any seven-step program or our own power. The transformation comes from Christ.

CHOOSING A LIFE OF LOVE

Real life love is a decision, not a feeling. By making the decision to live in love and exemplify love in your life, you choose to reflect the wonderful nature of Christ. In order to love, you must first be loved by God. Here's how John describes our life under love by God:

> God is love. When we take up permanent residence in a life of love, we live in God and God lives in us. This way, love has the run of the house, becomes at home and mature in us, so that we're free of worry on Judgment Day—our standing in the world is identical with Christ's. There is no room in love for fear. Well-formed love banishes fear. Since fear is crippling, a fearful life—fear of death, fear of judgment—is one not yet fully formed in love. (1 John 3:17–18)

When we decide to take up residence in a life of real love, our old self passes away. Our old love habits that were toxic and corrupt become suddenly null and void. Before we know it, anger is told to leave. Fear is told to leave. Judgment is told to leave. Abuse is told to leave. Abandonment is told to leave. Substance abuse is told to leave. Lust is told to leave. Pain is told to leave. Jesus revokes their ability to take up residence in your heart. And He moves in and becomes your new roommate.

When you make the decision to open your heart to Christ, to open your heart to love, you become plugged into a pure and clean power source. Instead of being plugged into your previous struggles of the flesh (we all have them), we are now plugged into Jesus. And in Jesus, struggles lose their power.

Like branches filled with green, healthy leaves that are

connected to a strong and healthy tree trunk, so are we connected to Christ when we decide to commit to him.

> I am the Vine, you are the branches. When you're joined with me and I with you, the relation intimate and organic, the harvest is sure to be abundant. Separated, you can't produce a thing. Anyone who separates from me is deadwood, gathered up and thrown on the bonfire. But if you make yourselves at home with me and my words are at home in you, you can be sure that whatever you ask will be listened to and acted upon. (John 15:5–8)

If we are plugged into a healthy vine, we start to become healthy. And we can begin to build a solid foundation of love in Christ. But things are a little tricky: We have to decide to do that. Here's where these seven principles begin to take center stage. When you see the words "real life love is a decision, not a feeling," and you're still a bit fuzzy on where to actually begin making decisions, consider the seven points I cover in this book.

1. We *decide to honor* the people in our life like the incredible creations they truly are. Each and every person we meet, including ourselves, is a one-of-a-kind masterpiece, worth more than anything else in the world. We need to pray, "Lord, help me to see the people in my life as who you created them to be. Reveal to me their distinctive traits that make them special to You. Help me to honor them like I would rare and precious gold bricks." Here's what Paul

says to the church in Rome about loving in this way: "Love from the center of who you are; don't fake it. Run for dear life from evil; hold on for dear life to good. Be good friends who love deeply; practice playing second fiddle" (Rom. 12:10).

2. We *decide to decrease anger* in our heart. Anger will do nothing but destroy us from the inside out. In fact, making the decision to stay angry with someone is like drinking poison and hoping the other person gets sick. We need to pray, "Lord, if there is any anger in me, get it out! I don't want it. Whisper to my heart whom or what I am angry with. Help me see them or the situation so I can begin to reverse the process. Help me do that, oh Lord! For I want to be rid of this pain and heaviness." Look at what Jesus compares anger to.

You're familiar with the command to the ancients, "Do not murder." I'm telling you that anyone who is so much as angry with a brother or sister is guilty of murder. Carelessly call a brother "idiot!" and you just might find yourself hauled into court. Thoughtlessly yell "stupid!" at a sister and you are on the brink of hellfire. The simple moral fact is that words kill. (Matthew 5:22)

3. We *decide to forgive*, not to continue in rage and anger. Making the decision not to forgive is equivalent to murdering your soul. Anger doesn't murder the soul of the person with whom you're upset. All the damage is done to you.

And when your soul is on life support, barely hanging on, anger then decides to come after the ones you love, tearing down their souls for fun. But you can put anger in jail and heal yourself by choosing to forgive. Forgiveness is an ally, not a sign of weakness. We need to pray, "Lord, help me in my anger by making my heart tender to forgiveness. I refuse to allow myself to be subject to the consequences of my anger and bitter feelings. I know it does me no good and blocks your love from entering my heart and mind. Help me forgive my offenders and their offenses, like You forgave me of mine."

Paul so eloquently describes this process in his letter to the church in Colossae.

So, chosen by God for this new life of love, dress in the wardrobe God picked out for you: compassion, kindness, humility, quiet strength, discipline. Be even-tempered, content with second place, quick to forgive an offense. Forgive as quickly and completely as the Master forgave you. And regardless of what else you put on, wear love. It's your basic, all-purpose garment. Never be without it. (Colossians 3:13–14)

4. We *decide to meditate on God's Word*, and with it open the gates for the transformative teaching and insights that can change our relationships. The Word of God is alive, more powerful and sharper than a two-edged sword. If something is that powerful, don't you think it can change and have a positive impact on just about anything? People

often equate the Word of God with the help we need to get us through daily life and fight our spiritual battles, but many forget to use it to fight one of the most important battles of all: the battle for our relationships. Stop using a foam noodle to fight off attacks on your relationships and start using the powerful weapon of God.

We need to pray, "Lord, confide in me Your precious Words. I open up my heart, mind, and will to begin learning all that you have to say through Your Scripture. Teach me the ways of love through Your Word. Show me what I need to begin doing, seeking, and being in my Scripture reading today. Transform me through the verses and teaching you have prepared for me."

Here's what Paul teaches the Hebrews about God's Word:

God means what he says. What he says goes. His powerful Word is sharp as a surgeon's scalpel, cutting through everything, whether doubt or defense, laying us open to listen and obey. Nothing and no one is impervious to God's Word. We can't get away from it—no matter what. (Hebrews 4:12–13)

5. We *decide to celebrate our trials* in every aspect of life. Life is full of hard times. Life isn't short on punches and jabs. Life doesn't hold back on woes and hardships. But Jesus doesn't hold back on the blessings we can receive from the trials life has to offer. Trials take a serious toll on our relationships. And relationships tend to be a major cause

of trials. If Jesus promises we'll face them, we better learn how to celebrate them. We need to start praying something like this: "Lord, you tell me daily that trials are coming my way. While I wish they were few and far between, I pray that you help me discover what treasures you have hidden in these messes. Give me the strength and strong will to keep paddling when I'm in the eye of the hurricane force winds. Get me to the other side, oh Lord! And my reward is always more of Your love, grace, peace, and endurance."

Paul encourages the ancient Christians in Rome with this same way of thinking.

There's more to come: We continue to shout our praise even when we're hemmed in with troubles, because we know how troubles can develop passionate patience in us, and how that patience in turn forges the tempered steel of virtue, keeping us alert for whatever God will do next. In alert expectancy such as this, we're never left feeling shortchanged. Quite the contrary—we can't round up enough containers to hold everything God generously pours into our lives through the Holy Spirit! (Romans 5:3–5)

6. We *decide to be a servant.* Once we give up on putting our needs first, our desires first, our preferences first, and our comforts first, and instead begin putting others first, our relationships will begin to change for the best. Living a life of servanthood and deciding to serve people in the way they most

want and need to be served is like an incubator for change and love. We need to pray, "Lord, help me to die to myself and help me live for others. Rid me of this need to put myself first and help me start serving the people in my life. Help me to also be sensitive to the needs of others in my environment. Put people through whom You want to demonstrate Your love in my path, so I can begin practicing serving them like You would."

Paul, a noble servant to the early church, looked at life this way:

I've never, as you so well know, had any taste for wealth or fashion. With these bare hands I took care of my own basic needs and those who worked with me. In everything I've done, I have demonstrated to you how necessary it is to work on behalf of the weak and not exploit them. You'll not likely go wrong here if you keep remembering that our Master said, "You're far happier *giving* than getting." (Acts 20:35, emphasis added)

7. We *decide to understand others*. God created each of us to have a unique and special personality. It's our responsibility to begin understanding those personalities—the way we tick and how to live and communicate with one another. We need to pray, "Lord, thank you for creating me with a personality that is unlike anyone else's in this world. Thank you for my strengths and weaknesses. They

both help and shape me to be a better person. Help me to be sensitive to others' personalities and their strengths and weaknesses. Give me the wisdom to understand people in regard to their personality."

Paul encouraged the Ephesians to understand one another and work through their differences.

> In light of all this, here's what I want you to do. While I'm locked up here, a prisoner for the Master, I want you to get out there and walk—better yet, run!—on the road God called you to travel. I don't want any of you sitting around on your hands. I don't want anyone strolling off, down some path that goes nowhere. And mark that you do this with humility and discipline— not in fits and starts, but steadily, pouring yourselves out for each other in acts of love, alert at *noticing differences* and quick at *mending fences*. (Ephesians 4:1–3, emphases added)

CALLED TO LOVE

We are called to a higher purpose, to love unconditionally first our Savior and then others. There isn't any room for something in between. The time to start loving is now. Because if we don't, then who are we to call ourselves God's children?

John challenges us with this:

We, though, are going to love—love and be loved. First we were loved, now we love. He loved us first. If anyone boasts, "I love God," and goes right on hating his brother or sister, thinking nothing of it, he is a liar. If he won't love the person he can see, how can he love the God he can't see? The command we have from Christ is blunt: Loving God includes loving people. You've got to love both. (1 John 4:19–21)

Now we love. It is our turn to begin exemplifying what Christ did for us. Remember what I said in the beginning of this book about Dr. Caroline Leaf's research on when our brain is operating at its full capacity, running on all four cylinders? It's when we are *loving* at our highest capacity. When we are loving for real, we are complete.

On May 18, 2018, the world watched as Meghan Markle, an American actress, married England's Prince Harry in a spectacular ceremony that had every woman in the world swooning. Her dress was elegant and simple. St. George's Chapel at the royal family's estate in Windsor was teeming with elegance. Celebrities like Oprah Winfrey, George and Amal Clooney, and tennis star Serena Williams as well as countless other famous people sat in pews as the newly appointed Duke and Duchess of Sussex said their vows. But with all that star power, one unlikely guest would steal the show. Asked to deliver the sermon, Reverend Michael Curry, the presiding bishop and primate of the Episcopal Church, reminded the world of the true magnitude of what this couple was becoming a symbol of to the world: a symbol of the power of love.

...Think and imagine a world where love is the way. When love is the way, then no child will go to bed hungry in this world ever again. When love is the way, we will let justice roll down like a mighty stream and righteousness like an ever-flowing brook. When love is the way, poverty will become history. When love is the way, the earth will be a sanctuary. When love is the way, we will lay down our swords and shields, down by the riverside, to study war no more. When love is the way, there's plenty good room, plenty good room for all of God's children. Because when love is the way, we actually treat each other, well, like we are actually family. When love is the way, we know that God is the source of us all and we are brothers and sisters, children of God.

Reverend Curry couldn't be more right. When love finds a way, people find their way too. Change occurs. Suffering endures no more. Relationships flourish. Peace is established. And the best part is you don't have to be a prince or princess to find this love. We each, just the same, have the ability to invite love to flow through our veins and relationships. And when we are loving others to the best of our ability, we are living like what we were always meant to be—like Christ. That's the whole point, right? Decades before the wedding of Prince Harry and Meghan Markle, C. S. Lewis, the great Christian author and thinker, wrote in *Mere Christianity* (emphasis added):

> We shall love the Father as He does and the Holy Ghost will arise in us. He came to this world and became a man in order to spread to other men the kind of life He has—by what I call "good infection." Every Christian is to become *a little Christ*. The whole purpose of becoming a Christian is simply nothing else.

By turning to Jesus, we are infected with love. In our pursuit of living the Christian life, we accomplish this important task of becoming like Christ by choosing to be infected by love over hate. We choose an infection of love over being affected by conflict. We choose an infection of love over being affected by our issues. We choose an infection of love over being affected by comfort. We choose an infection of love over being affected by generational sin. We choose to be an infection of love over being affected by divorce. We choose Jesus every time. We choose to mimic His extravagant love. Then, and only then, will our relationships begin to change for better or the best.

Then, and all of a sudden, you feel it. As if waking up early in the morning during a long car ride through the dark night, you feel the delicate warm light of the new day on your face. You look out, and you are no longer where you were. Surrounded by a beautiful and colorful sunrise, you are in a new place, with new horizons and a new day.

The old has passed away. The new has come. Love has entered your heart. Love has emerged in your relationships. Welcome to *real life love*.

ACKNOWLEDGMENTS

I once heard a famous fiction writer say that writing your first book is like trying to push several large boulders up a steep hill. It's rough, heavy, soul-searching, empowering, and at times punishing. But sometimes, if you're lucky, the most remarkable people come alongside you not only to offer their help, encouragement, and love, but to put their shoulder to the boulder and help move it forward. I have been fortunate to have multiple people—friends, family, and mentors—offer their incredible assistance on this book. With my whole heart, I'd like to thank my fellow boulder pushers.

Les, without your support and generosity, this book would still be a pipe dream. Thanks not only for helping me get this book off the ground, but for lending your research and hard-earned insights to this project. Your tremendous wisdom shines through every part of this book. I'm grateful to have you in my corner.

Dad, you are my hero, protector, teacher, counselor, and literary agent. What a combination! Thanks for being the greatest dad a son could ask for. You have always taught me to follow my dreams. This book is a testament to that advice.

Mom, I wouldn't be here without you. From day one, you have been my best friend, greatest encourager, spiritual role model, and my own personal motivational speaker. Tony Robbins has nothing on you! You love me no matter what. There's not a day that goes by when I don't think I'm the luckiest guy in the world to have a mom like you.

Hannah and Zoie, I read a quote once that said, "Siblings are the people we practice on, the people who teach us about fairness and cooperation and kindness and caring." You both have taught me so much and showed me love even when I didn't deserve it. My life is complete with you in it. My real life princesses.

Grammy and Nanny, my precious grandmothers, I dedicated this book to your husbands, my grandfathers. But I would argue that if I asked them both, they would urge me to swap out their names and put yours. Thanks for giving me the best parents. Their love started with your love. A love that I treasure deeply. And a love that I am so thankful for every day.

Keren, from our first phone call, I knew instantly you were a writer's answer to a prayer. Thanks for challenging me to be real and showing me that this book wasn't an accident. It was a calling. Your belief in me has made all the difference with this project. Your eloquence and wisdom made this book better.

Rolf, you gave my grandpa the chance to achieve some

of his biggest publishing dreams. Now, all these years later, you've given me the same gift. A gift that I don't take lightly. Thanks for giving me a publishing home. And the best folks to work with.

Grace, Emily, Bob, Janet, Patsy, Rudy, and the entire Hachette team, if people only knew the stuff you did to get this book in their hands! All your hard work inspired me to work harder. Thanks for being the best of the best at what you do.

Rob, Jordyn, Jakob, Bradley, Kate, Violet, Lexy, Megan, Wynne, Liz, Bryan, and Sue, books are only as good as their advanced readers. Luckily, I was blessed with the very best. This book and its content stand on your shoulders. Thank you.

Nadia, you are an extraordinary friend. Thanks for all the lunches, a beautiful office space, stimulating conversation, and endless encouragement and kindness. Your genuine, sweet spirit and world-changing compassion inspire me every day. If more people honored each other like you have honored me, this world would be a greater place.

Marcus and Shannon, they say that friends are the family you choose. How did I get so blessed to have such wonderful family like you and your sons? Thanks for the incredible encouragement, late-night chats, delicious turkey sandwiches, and a comfy guest room and for teaching me what it looks like to love and serve someone like yourself.

President Taylor, Dr. Pace, Ms. Booze, Dr. Kelton, Mrs. Pace-Miller, Dr. Stanek, Jon, Wanda, and the entire Evangel University community, I am indebted to you. To say that you helped me hone my craft, facilitated spiritual growth, introduced me to my passion, and groomed me to rise to the occasion with nothing but my best would be an understatement. I am a better man because of each of you.

Last, but certainly not least, to my Lord Jesus. Thank You for trusting me with this message. You have never let me down. Your faithfulness sustains me through it all. The strength, guidance, love, hope, blessings, and grace You give me every day never cease to blow me away. Every day in Your service is an adventure that I wouldn't trade for the world. I give You all the praise.

ABOUT THE AUTHOR

MICHAEL GIBSON is an Emmy® Award–winning television personality, author, and communicator. His popular blog and podcast help thousands learn how to have relationships that count. As the grandson of relationship expert and best-selling author Gary Smalley, Michael uses his knowledge and experiences from speaking alongside his grandpa at his conferences since he was ten years old and growing up as the son of marriage pastors to call others into deeper, fuller relationships. He calls the Ozark Mountains of Missouri home. Find out more at MichaelGibson.org.

Michael loves connecting with his readers. You can email him at michael@michaelgibson.org or connect with him on Facebook @theMichaelGibson, Twitter @MichaelTGibson, or Instagram @michaeltgibson.

Michael is also available to engage in person with your gathering, business, or audience. He brings to the table an inspiring message of love and learning how to have healthy relationships. He also puts on an incredible seminar that he hosts with his dad called *Momentous*. For more information on inviting Michael to speak, visit MichaelGibson.org/Speaking.